30
Novelty
Architecture

PAGE ONE

Architecture • City • Culture

The beauty of life stems from the exploration and discovery by city dwellers. With continuous cultural development, the bonding between man and city has become closer; and the connection between man and architecture has also become inseparable. Cities are not just places in which people live, but also a platform on which history and culture are passed on.

Some suggested that a city's autobiography is written by the architectures therein; whilst others might believe that architectures resemble mini-cities, and cities embody the extension of architectures. A city is formed by groups of architectures, which, at the same time, act as the core of the city. Different forms of architecture determine the city's characteristics. They feature the city's culture across various periods of time, represent the folkways, and most importantly, keep track of the city's development. Architecture is not just built upon its 'outer appearance', but also upon its historical background, cultural status as well as the allure it creates. It is perpetual, will remain over time and extend to the future.

Architecture is the product left behind by the passage of time. It significantly reflects the characteristics of society. As the world's economy, technology and culture develop rapidly, human beings have succeeded in making use of nature and gaining from within. Yet, growing population, overuse of resources, climate change, environmental pollution as well as ecological destruction are posing great threats to our lives and development. Thus, attaining sustainable development and protecting the environment

become a major task for architects.

Architecture is produced by a specific region or district. There is no such thing in the world as 'abstract architecture'; there is only concrete architecture, which is rooted in a substantial environment, and thus is very much restricted by the topographic and natural conditions of the area, as well as the landforms and other existing buildings in the city.

As some scholars put forward, architecture is an art of solidification. By 'solidification' it means the blending of racial culture, as well as the incarnation of folkways. The cultural characteristic of architecture lies in its dualism. Such dualism of architecture refers to material wealth as well as spiritual possession. It is both a result of technological advancement and a creation of art. If there is no culture in it, architecture can be said to be lifeless. This also applies to other constructions in the city. Within them, we should be able to feel an intense sense of culture, but not merely the modernized elements. However, modern architecture, either from the West or the East, is usually designed by similar architectural skills and spatial arrangements. During such process, the regional characteristics and traditional culture have been marginalized, and corroded by the beautiful packing of the modernized society and are gone forever. This is a disaster of the city's culture. The connotation of a fine building always prevails the building's functions perse. Every fine work should be able to portray certain spiritual connotation, and have high standards of cultural savor. There are a bunch of undying architectural works in each period of time in the history, and the cultural essence and artistic magical power always represent a certain historical period, and the nation's and people's spirit.

Architecture is a sign of culture and a solidified form of art. It exists for human beings, and is concurrently nourished by people's art and culture.

Contents

Location   Kobuchizawa, Japan
Clients   Risonare (Hoshino Resort)
Architects   Klein Dytham architecture
                  Astrid Klein, Mark Dytham,
                  Yoshinori Nishimura, Yukinari Hisayama
Landscape designer Studio On Site
Lighting designer   ICE
Structure engineer Arup Japan
Photos   Katsuhisa Kida
Total area   167 887 m²

Leaf Chapel

The Leaf Chapel, located in the Risonare Resort Hotel, has a fresh green background. The beautiful mount Fuji could be seen even from a distance. The Chapel is composed of two pieces of "leaves"—one is made of glass and the other is steel. The roof looks as if it is floating away from the earth and suspending on the water. The decorated glass in the form of a "leaf", resembles a shelf-structure supporting the roof. The edge of the leaf which is apart from the main branch becomes thinner and thinner, creating a feeling of the leaf's texture. The white steel "leaf" has 4 700 holes. Each hole is fixed with an acrylic plexiglass lens, which looks like an elegant lace on a bride's veil. When the light passes through the lens, it projects patterns on the white fabric in the interior of the construction. Along with the move of the sun, the projected patterns change accordingly, creating an extraordinary background for the wedding.

When the wedding ends, the groom flips over the bride's veil and kisses her. Then, the steel "leaf screen" will open magically to reveal the pool outside and the charming natural scenery to the visitors. Although the steel weighs 11 tons, it could be raised up quietly by the round column machines in 38 seconds, just like lifting up a piece of thin cloth.

The specially-chosen material forms a black decoration in the interior and makes the entire space become brighter and pure. Black wood is used to decorate the walls and black granites are used to cover the floor. Black benches, with its back made of acrylic acid can accommodate about 80 people. A beautiful green flower pattern is inserted in

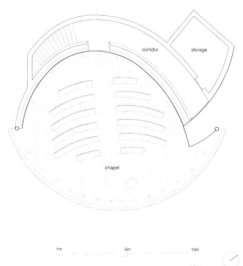

corridor   storage

chapel

1m   5m   10m

plan

the 20mm acrylic to create a soft affection. Viewing from the back of the chapel, facing the pool and looking through the opened screen, all this look like a lot of waterplants growing and floating in the pool. When the screen falls down, it seems like a big cluster flowers swaging on the white background. The flower, named Rempuksou with little yellow petal lines, has been chosen to be planted beside the little rivulet. It means "luck" in Chinese and is very suitable for wedding celebrations. When the ceremony approaches the end and the screen is opened, people attending the wedding can walk on the stone steps through the pool and arrive at the greenbelt to enjoy champagne and bread.

Holding a wedding ceremony in the leaf chapel under the moonlight enables you to enjoy the charming scenery. The flood-light shines through the lens in the screen and forms an elegant picture. Flipping open the screen, numerous candles are lit on the ground to lead guests to pass through the pool. When they are enjoying the champagne, the leaf chapel takes the moonlight as the background. When the screen is closed, a light will come out from the chapel, making it look like a beautiful lantern.

Location Kastrup

Purveyor Tarnby kommune

Architects White Arkitekter A/S

The design team Fredrik Pettersson (head of project)
Rasmus Skaarup, Pernille Vermund,
Goeran Wihl, Henrik Haremst, Johnny Gere

Engineer NIRAS Radgivende ingeniorer og
Planlaeggere A/S

Construction company Kobenhavns, Dykkerentreprise A/S

Photos Ole Haupt, White arkitekter, Erco Lighting

Kastrup Sea Bath

The Kastrup Sea Bath, extending from the Kastrup park directly to the Oresund Channel, becomes a bright and beautiful scenery and an integral component of this seacoast. The whole project includes the main construction on the water a new beach and a series of related service facilities, including toilets and dressing rooms for the disabled.

A wooden wharf is connected to a circular construction, and extends upwards until it is above the sea level. The end of the path is a 5-meter high diving platform. The red lignum vitae are used as the main material because of its high resistance against marine corrosion. The frames of this sea bath are very thin and are about 1 meter higher than the water. The supporting parts of this construction can be seen clearly. The whole project includes 870sqm wooden boards, 70sqm dressing facilities and 90sqm on shore servicing facilities.

The sea bath, as a dynamic sculpture, could be seen from the seashore, ocean and sky. When people visit it, the outline of the side will change gently with different angles of view. The round structure gathers the interior spaces to be sheltered from the wind and to gather light. The entrance of the building is open to the land and connected with the beach, making it convenient for visitors to enter. Along the wharf, there is a row of connected benches providing visitors with more space for rest and leisure.

The most important concept of this project's design is that it is designed as a public

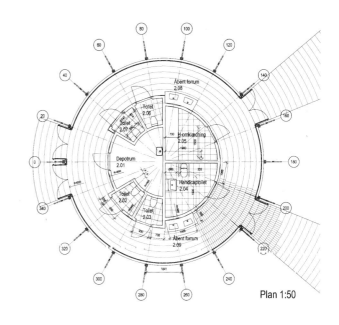

Plan 1:50

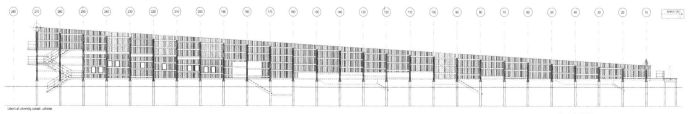

Udsnit af udvendig opstalt, udfoldet.

20

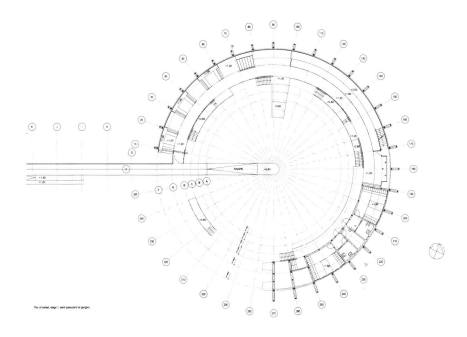

Plan af sebad, etage 1, samt planudsnit af gangbro.

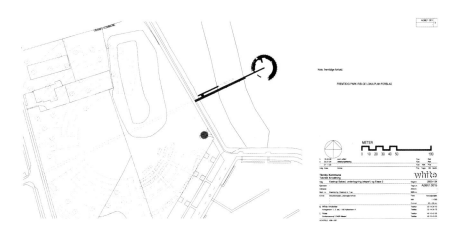

Note, fremtidige forhold.

FREMTIDIG PARK IFØLGE LOKALPLAN FORSLAG

METER
0 10 20 30 40 50   100

Tårnby Kommune
Teknisk forvaltning   white

Kastrup Søbad, underbygning (etape1) og Etape 2

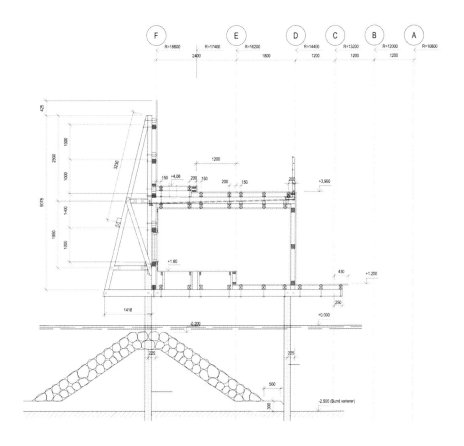

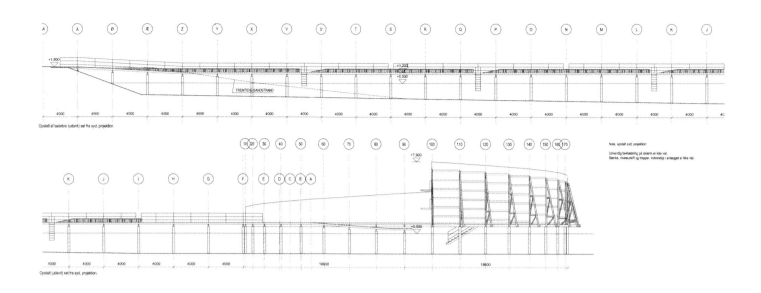

Opstalt af badebro (udsnit) set fra syd, projektion.

Note, opstalt syd, projektion:

Udvendig beklædning på skærm er ikke vist.
Bænke, niveauskift og trapper, indvendig i anlægget er ikke vist.

Opstalt (udsnit) set fra syd, projektion.

24

place which is free for entry the whole day. The design pursues the non-traditional structure for experiencing different kind of sports. There is a quiet place for swimming in the night as well as a place for exciting sports and competitions. The ramp and the other specially-designed facilities enable those who do not like sports to find the things they can also enjoy in the sea bath.

Apart from its usual illumination function and ensuring of the safety of tourists, the illumination of Kastrup sea bath also provides an extraordinary experience in the night and in the long polar-night season for visitors. All lights are from Erco Lighting and the design of the lighting system takes the sculpture design into account. The most important part is a series of huge, upper-lit lamps, which lit the half-circular walls inside. The light reflected from the walls illuminates the entire basin-liked place. People are able to enjoy the dynamic appearance from the neighborhood. When the reflected light becomes the brightest, it forms a sharp comparison with the blue light which shoots from the open-staircase and the back of the diving platform. Other main illumination facilities are the two rows LED which are arranged along the wharf.

HydraPier Exhibition Hall

Asymptote Architecture was commissioned to design a municipal exhibition hall called the HydraPier exhibition hall which is located at the Floriade 2002 World Horticultural Exhibition host city Haarlemmermeer.

The idyllic scenery of HydraPier contrasts sharply with the airplanes from the nearby Schipol Airport and the heavy traffic on the suburb highway. In the 19th century, the Haarlemmermeer area is laid 5 meters below than the horizon, until 150 years ago, where the water had dried and the land appeared. Thanks to the 19th century's dam and pumping station which still exist today, the low land has successfully to transformed into a place for people to live. Located at the lakeside, the HydraPier marks the clear slight boundary betwwen the land and the water. In order to show the rich history in this area, the water in the lake has been pumped over to the hall roof and then falled down from the "water walls", which is built vertically on the two sides of the hall, creating a marvellous view.

The HydraPier is located at a roof-covered scenery spot, which is near to the Haarlemmermeer forest. It has also become a connecting bridge between the two water walls. Otherwise it is also a multimedia center, which rises above the lake surface and is surrounded by a huge wharf. The landscape design therein includes two metal planes, which is built to match the interior and the exterior pools and designed into a special shape. The shell of planes is covered by flowing water and inclined toward the hall. The landscape of two planes incarnates the unification of nature with science and technology. Visitors enter this place from a suspended glass pool, which is 5 meters high and

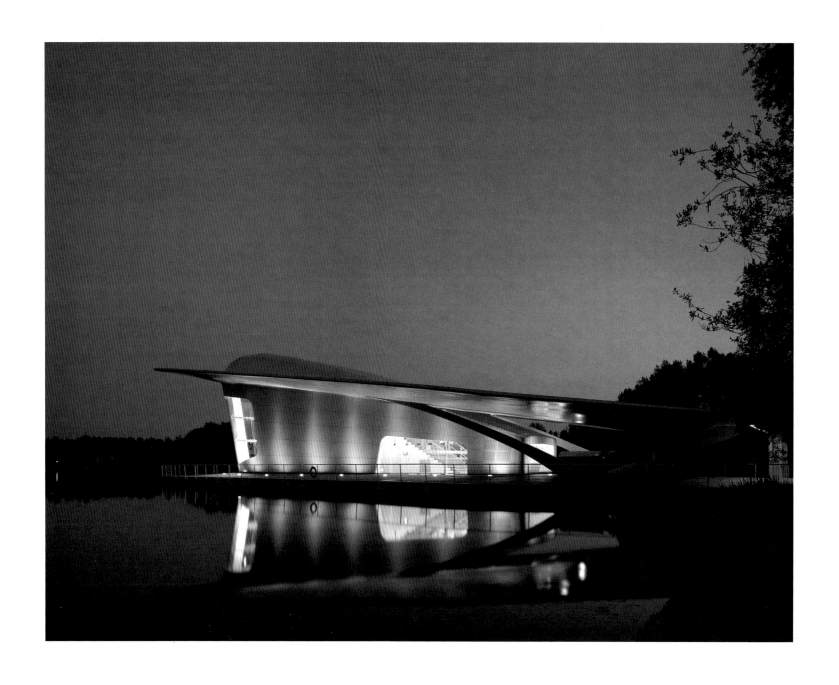

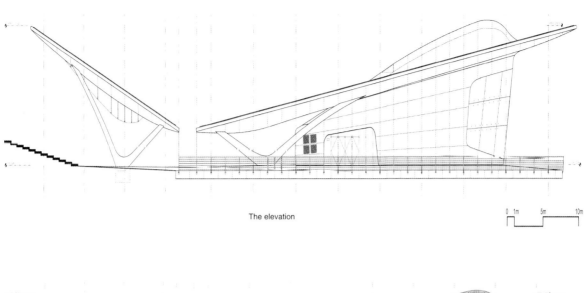

The elevation

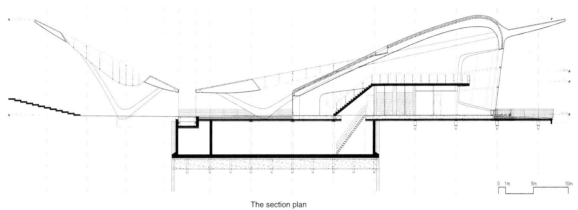

The section plan

symbolises the original horizontal level. The pumping system makes water wash out constantly on the surface of the aluminum hall. This controlled flowing integrates with the plane's wing structure, and creates a bright glistening outside the wall that resembles flowing water. The appearance of the hall changes with time. In daytime, visitors who pass by the hall through planes or those who are standing on the ground can see the roof highly raised upwards, just as the flowing water reflects the sky. At night, the roof becomes a lamp-house of light and projected images. From the bottom of the slick glass in the pool as well as the lower part of the roof's opening, the flowing water could be seen clearly. The broad space is formed by massive draining water and the decreased sea level. It also reminds the visitors of the natural environment of the HydraPier that is operated by human management.

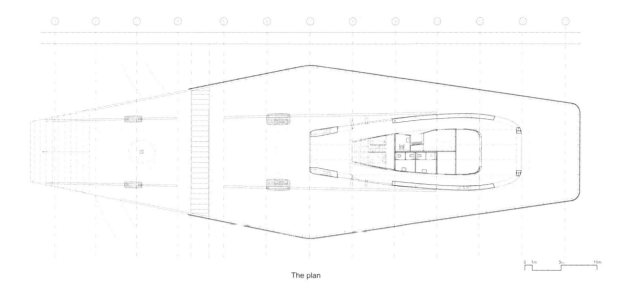

The plan

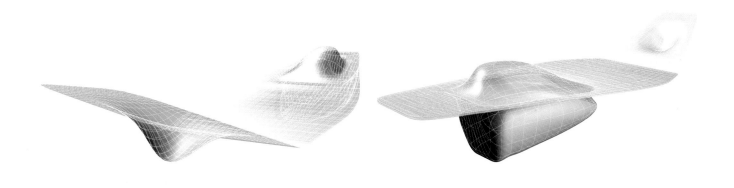

Location YAKSOO park, Korea

Architects Liujian+Jinhuiting (株) Sisang construction, Myungji college faculty of architecture

Structure design (株)Tokugawa engineering

Exhibition design Hejing design

Total area 1 600 m²

Structure Reinforced concrete

Museum of Solo Island, Korea

The Three Peaks Island (Solo Island) Museum is built on the Pentagon Island (Yuling Island) and connected with the existing local feed hall of the YAKOO park and the newly bulit ropeway facilities.

The natural mountains, hillsides, villages are floating down from the Saint peak and form seveal repeated lines. The sea represents the borderline of the territory, which will be recorded from generation to generation. The Solo Island symbolizes the achromatic tree sides of the three peaks, it also leads people to imagine the central hall designing shape—the sunrise from the East Ocean.

This symbolic meaning and space together forms the Solo Island Museum.

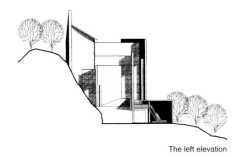

The left elevation

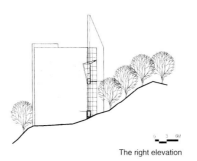

The right elevation

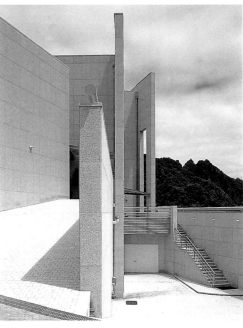

36

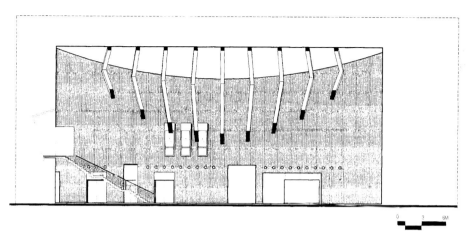

The interior wall elevation of central hall

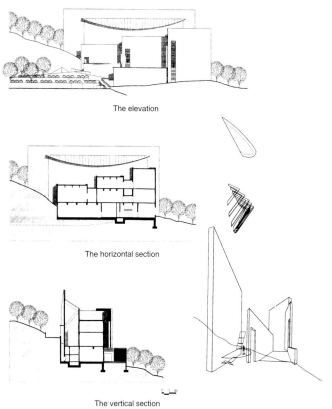

The elevation

The horizontal section

The vertical section

Designer   Fentress Bradburn Architects Ltd
Clients   Buffalo Bill Historical Center, Wyoming, US
The main contractor   Jacobsen Construction Company
The project manager   WOZ Group
Civil engineer & landsacple architect   Fischer & Associates
The structure engineer   Richard Weingardt Consultants
Electrical engineer   M&E CTA
Exhibition designer   DMCB (Primary), Gensler, WOED
The area   1 213 m²
Photos   Chip Raches

Draper Museum of Natural History, US

The Buffalo Bill Historical Center is regarded as the best theme museum in western America. It is located on a cliff of northeast Wyoming, facing the Shoshone River and is 52 miles away from the eastern entrance of Yellowstone National Park. This historical center requires the architects to ceate a new long–lasting image for the building. It includes the essence of western America, which is not comparable with other places in America, since its image is redefined by commemorative and heroic style.

The Draper Museum of Natural History is the last unit which fully portrays the characteristics of the West. It is added to the central four museums that are famous in the world, namely, the Whitney west Art Corridor, the Buffalo Bill Museum, the Indian Plain Museum and the Koudi Weapon Museum.

The Fentress Bradburn Arhitect provided the plan for the Draper Museum's design, fulfilling the requirements of the project by adopting a vivid style and reflecting the scen–

ery of the neighbor environment. Each step of designing work of the new museum and the historical center is to boost the Yellowstone Park's traveling industry, as well as stimulating people's interests in natural local and national history.

It could be seen from the plan or the elevation that the wing building of the Draper Museum contrasts with the Weapon Museum. Its round shape surrounds the drop-down area in the main entrance, breaking the center's linear structure. The interior resembles a mini New York Guggenheim Museum Bilbao. Four quarter of the round cubes go downwards directly from the main floor and symbolize the natural landscape of the Yellowstone Park area-from the peak of Alps, acrossing the forest lawn, reaching the plain in the bottom.

The interactive exhibits, advanced setting and atmospheric light in the museum are designed according to the humanistic perspective create an interesting environment for the old and young.

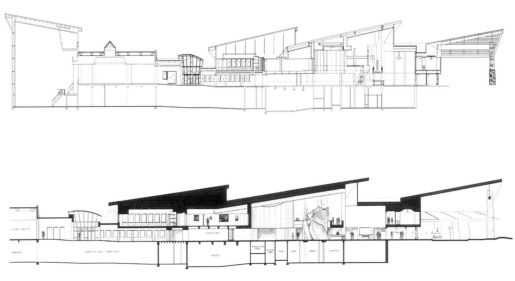

The section plan

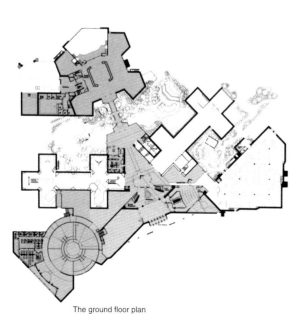

The ground floor plan

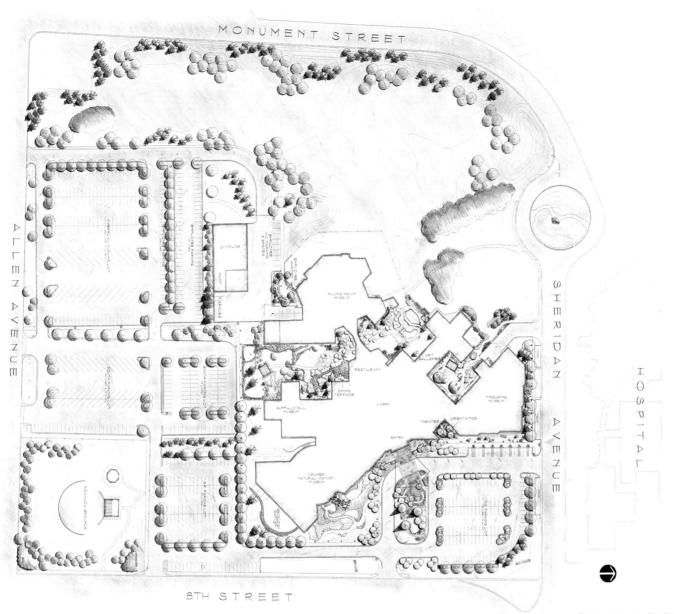

The layout drawing: The Buffalo Bill Historical Center is composed by the Draper Museum of Natural History, the Whitney West Art Corridor, the Buffalo Bill Museum, the Indian Plain Museum and the Koudi Weapon Museum

The east elevation

The south elevation

Clients Department of Administrative and Information Services on behalf of Department of Education and Children's Services, South Australia

Architects MGT Canberra Architects (Guida Moseley Brown Architects), Russell & Yelland Architects

Designing Harold Guida

Administrative partner Tim Brown

Design manager Stephen Schrapel

The design team Pamille Berg, Justine Cox, Pero Dimcev, Wayne Henkel, Andrew McKenna

The design team John Anesbury, Meredith Harrison, John Held, John Mau, Helen Vaughan

Photos John Gollings, Steve Rendoulis, Harold Guida

Mawson Lakes School, South Australia

The Mawson Lakes School, which is next to the South Australian University, the Technology Garden and the elder students' new dormitory, took into account students' lifelong learning, and thus adopted a new design which enables the students to use it for the rest of their lives. In the 12th century, to children aged 3 to 13, the first stage of learning in school is a kind of broad exploration of knowledge. Hence, designers had consulted more than 40 relevant people and organizations before the commencement of the design.

The work site is one half smaller than other similar schools. The school is allowed to use the community outdoor activity areas and facilities. It has installed fences in the place facing the urban center. A series of green belts have been arranged in the school garden and the open space. The Dry Creek (a rill) also has been kept. Four "Family Units" have been built on the north–south hunched belt to serve 110 students.All the doors of the Family Units face the garden on the North, and they have unique windows and clapboards which are connected to the ladder garden. Walking forward along the garden, we can see the four "family unit" which are linear and they give the school a sensation of sculpture. The other two constructions are built symmetrically with the northern entrance and a samll square is formed in the middle.

The designers made an attempt to make the design simple, interactive and able to reflect the functions of family units through making full use of natural light (solar energy) and the natural ventilation. The height of the single–layer is extended by inclined roofs and strengthened by the use of solar energy chimney.

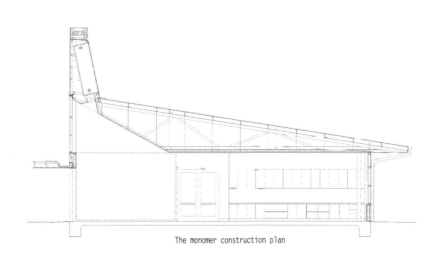

The monomer construction plan

The changing order of the layout follows the changes of Kerbsides. The use of different materials in the garden fences, together with the unique shape of the windows in "family units", gives a special experience to the passengers. There is a huge fiberglass which has been fixed into one wall of the garden and the end of "school's axes". The "green school cabin" together with other free combinations of contructions integrates into the entire layout of the city.

The administrative building faces the small square and is very easy to be seen. It is very convenient for people to observe the school personnel going in and out. The buffets and activity room are located at the center, both of which can be seen easily from the hunched belt, the garden and the open spaces of the school and all of them form a united image.

Inside the school, all constructions are designed with the concept of sustainable development. It makes use of natural ventilation and guarantees the fresh air circulation and effective management of warming and cooling in rooms with the use of "heat chimney" and its pipes. The details of design reveal the suitable structure and the use of materials, which resembles a part of study plan. Then, students are able to take the monitoring and changing the environment as a part of their learning plan.

The plan

Location   Seattle, USA
Clients   The Seattle Public Library
Architects   OMA/LMN-A Joint Venture
Engineer   Arup / Magnusson Klemencic Associates
The plan   Courtesy OMA
Photos   Fred Housel; Courtesy SPL
                  Pragnesh Parikh photography OMA/LMN
                  Architects, Philippe Ruault
Text   Joshua Ramus
Acoustics consultant Michael Yantis Associates
ADA   McGuire Associates
Artist   Ann Hamilton, Gary Hill, Tony Oursler
Surroundings design   Bruce Mau Design
Elevation design Dewhurst Macfarlane & Partners
Hardware   Gordon Adams Consulting
Interior design   OMA/LMN; Inside/Outside
Landscape design Inside/Outside; Jones & Jones
Safety consultant Pielow Fair Associates
Lighting design   Kugler Tillotson Associates
Elevator   HKA Elevator Consulting

Seattle Central Library

The project covers 38 300sqm in total, and some 33 700sqm comprises: a head–quarters office, a reading room, an information room, a meeting room, a leisure zone, staff offices, child activity zone and the hall; whist the rest 4 600sqm is for parking. The project has obtained the AIA Award 2005 and also has also been named "the best Library Archi–tecture" by the American Library Association.

The library could be said as the last indisputable protective line in the moral domain. The moral strength of library is connected with the value of the books–the library itself is a fortress, and the librarians are the bodyguards.

The survival of the library seems to have been threatened by the emergence of the new mediums and its growing prevalence. The library has seemingly become a fortress which could be intruded by new technologies at any moment. In this myth, electronic technology becomes a barbarian which exists everywhere. Its uncontrolled latency has led to the disappearance of order, tradition and culture. In that case, the library becomes the protective and moral language, which symbolizes a kind of extraordinary mission, social responsibility and principle.

Library seems to be antique; yet it is a public area in which the bottom–line of morality is still upheld and free and public service is provided. We are to redefine library through designing, making it a place which is not merely for book collection, but also information storage. Inside it, all mediums, either modern or traditional ones, are equal and legitimate. In this age of information, the presence all mediums is indispensable in managing the

content conveyed by the mediums, renovating the vigor of the library.

The flexibility of modern libraries tells us that an multi−function floor is necessary. People could organize kinds of activities here. Those activities are not separate, and there is no independency between rooms and private spaces. In fact, this means in the open day, the bookshelves will arrange a wide space for reading. Yet, due to the increasing size of the collection, the public space is occupied unavoidably. After all, this so−called "flexibility" will just make no difference to the library from any other medium.

When compared with the current vague flexibility, the library can better manage the space, such that every space can be specially renovated according to its own functions and usage. Adding flexibility to every single space is workable, and it would not affect the usage of other spaces and areas.

Our design is to rearrange and furnish the seemingly uncontrollable items and medium in the library, and group them into different categories, including five "stable groups" and four "unstable groups". Each platform is a function block, which is designed according to the construction space, and also is equipped according to its functions. This is because each plat−

form should be specially designed according to its function, size, flexibility, conductivity, color, structure and average effective pressure.

The space in between each platform can be used as the 'exchange level'. The exchange level is a place for the librarians to provide communication service. In between different platforms, spaces are designed as the workplace, interactive zone and leisure place.

The library spiral floor distribution (Book spiral) is a little similar to the Dewey books classification, which collects all the books as a long continual belt, and arranges the books from 000 to 999. Then, various items collected together are like an organism. Each subject is related to the others, it takes up some belt−shaped space but it is not separated completely. In the Seattle Library, the spiral book shelter has 6 233 bookshelves which have collected 780 000 books, guaranteeing a total of 1 450 000 books can be collected without needing additional bookshelves. The information exchange room becomes a place for librarians to interact and exchange information, and provide help for the readers. It amalgamates the accumulated human and technological resources in the library, enabling the readers to enter a world which is filled with information.

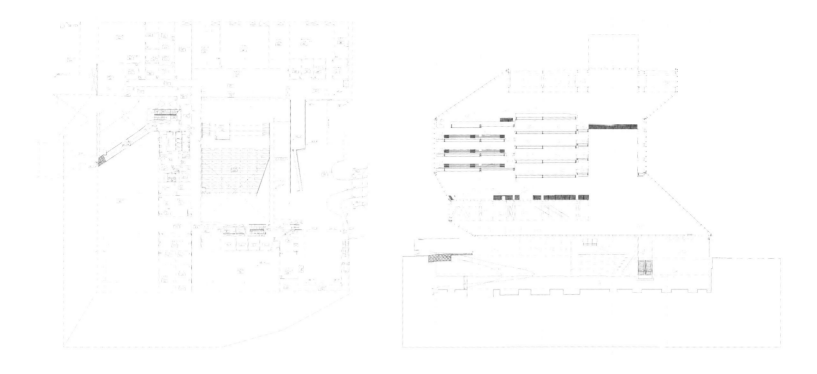

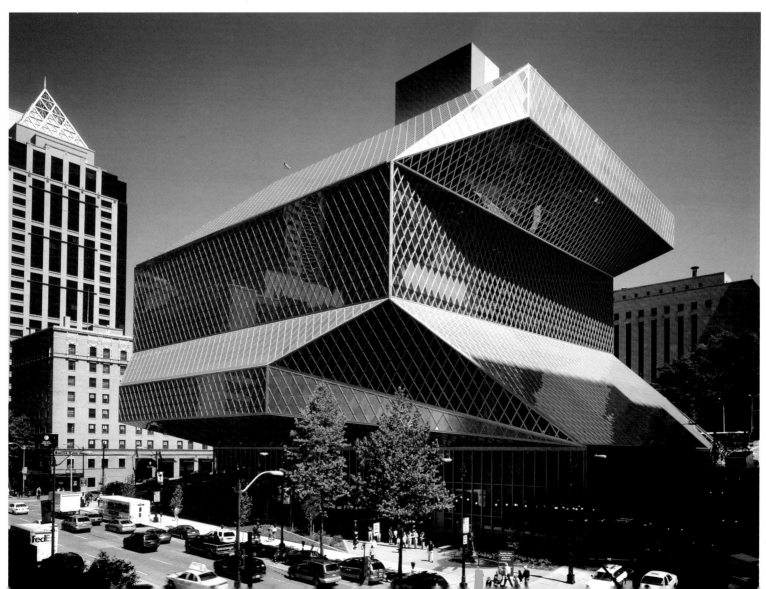

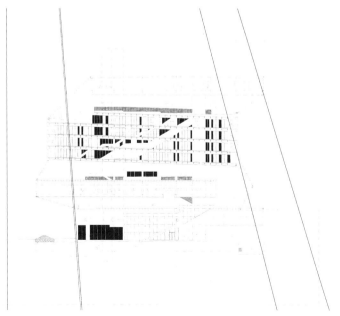

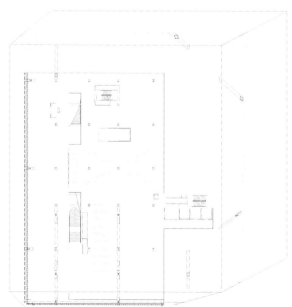

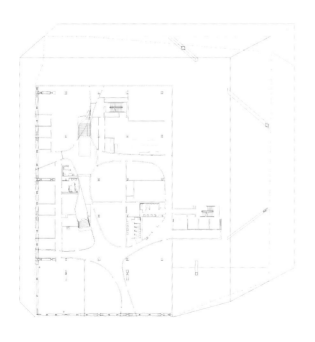

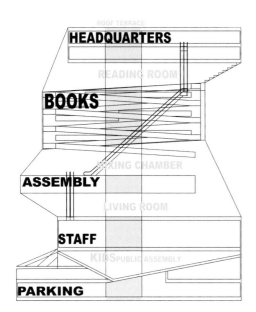

The research on the factors affecting every function and setup of the library

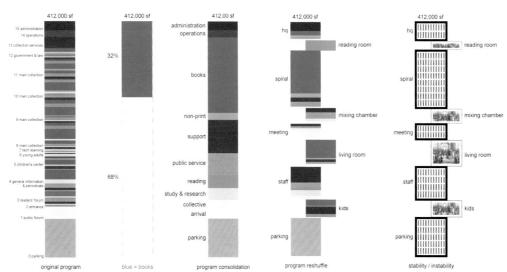

TRADITIONAL:

LIBRARIAN = 👤
KNOWLEDGE =

MIXING CHAMBER

SEATTLE:

LIBRARIAN = 👤
KNOWLEDGE –

BOOK SPIRAL

TRADITIONAL:

LIBRARIAN = 👤
PATRON = 👤

SEARCH TIME ELAPSED: 16 MINUTES

MIXING CHAMBER

SEATTLE:

LIBRARIAN = 👤
PATRON = 👤

BOOK SPIRAL

SEARCH TIME ELAPSED: 7 MINUTES

The comparison between the employment of librarians and the setup of their managing area and the effects on the readers between tra–ditional libraries and the Seattle Public library

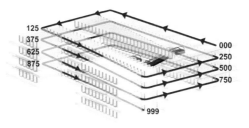

Library spiral floor (Book Spiral) schematic drawing

Location Vaughan, Ontario
Clients Vaughan Public Library Board
Architects Diamond and Schmitt Architects
Photos Steven Evans, Tom Arban

Pierre Berton Resource Library

The designing purpose of this library is to meet the increasing multi-cultural population as well as the escalating needs for information, culture, study and leisure. The Berton public library is a forerunner who always applies the latest technology to benefit the library users. Hence, a row of computers which is connected to the internet, words processing work station and CD-driver have been installed to satisfy the increasing demands.

Due to the continual requirement of science and technology development, the design has added flexibility to the library such that the readers are able to move from the traditional books to the internet workstation. In the leisure room, people can use the portable computer to enter the workstation. The computer laboratory can be used for teaching and doing research. And in the teens' zone, the "assignment zone" provides a computer workstation for readers and it is near to the reading desk, so readers can check out the explanation and assistance in the first place. The fixed wired and the wireless connection can be found everywhere, and the meeting room can be used for library and community activities.

The library comprises two floors, and the area is approximately 3 344sqm. The designing purpose is to make the library more eye-catching so that people can see it.

Along the Rutherford Road, the northern elevation is built with glass walls, so people outside can see all the activities in the building clearly. A double–floor net bar is viewable at the sides. It is like a kind of medium which is constructed in between the inside and outside. From the outside, the bar looks like a light tower; but for the readers from the inside, the room is the source of all the information. There is a hectic area on the ground floor, which comprises a leisure reading room and a child activity room. The first floor, which comprises a quiet study room, is used for research. The meeting and research room are built from middle of the huge building and stands up along the Rutherford Road. Thus, people are able to see the Boyd Conservation nearby.

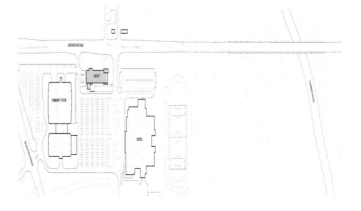

The orientation plan

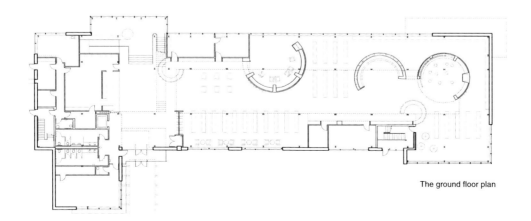

The ground floor plan

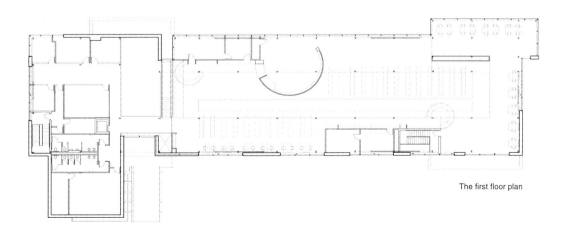

The first floor plan

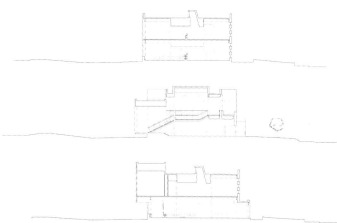

Location	Adelaide, South Australia
Clients	Department for Administrative and Information
	Services, South Australia onbehalf of Arts South
	Australia
Architects	MGT Architects, Canberra (Guida Moseley
	Brown Architects); Hassell Pty Ltd, Adelaide
Design partner	Harold Guida
Administrative partner	Tim Brown
Designer manager	Sieglinde Whittle
Designer	David Antcliff, Doug Brooks, Justine Cox,
	Michael Komnacki, Fiona Lynch, Paul Nihill,
	Robert Patat, Stephanie Simko, Shoba Thiruchelvam
Director	David Hassell
Designer	Jonathon Ash, Neroli Hutchinson, Michael
	Pearce, Birgit Stroeher, Terry Suey
	Bannyan Wood
Exhibition design	Pamille Berg Consulting Pty Ltd.
Art project	Kay Lawrence in association with John Nowland
Artist	Pantjiti McKenzie (Ernabella Arts Inc.)
Photos	John Gollings, Harold Guida

Redevelopment of Stata Library of South Australia

The project's purpose is to supply a modernized library with facilities for collection of books and reading, gather the latest information, the telecommunication technology and public activities and exhibition, and give a quality workspace for the staff and the administrators. The redevelopment project includes the reconstruction of some structural parts of the building, and it is hoped to attain the following aims: to create a flexible and enlarged space for readers, to install modernized telecommunication and safety facilities, to bring natural light into the reading room, such that the readers can see the landscape outside. Other newly installed facilities include: information zone, waiting zone, zones that are specially designed for personal collection and group study, as well as the outdoor reading chairs.

The redesigned library improved the security measures of collection zone. It also provides for readers a passage which in connected to the outside. Thus, it is very convenient for people to reach other spaces. One of the most noticeable parts of the redesign project is the newly built permanent exhibition hall for collection, which strengthened the functions of the resting room and meeting room, allowing the readers to acquire knowledge from the large collections. Likewise, the Ron Bollan newspaper reading zone inside the booking collection monitoring zone also provides with the public intact information via exhibition. It is to respect the renowned newspaper editor and to commemorate the contemporary field of journalism.

In the construction, the three buildings which compose the library have been given 'new appearances'. First, the Institute Building and Jervois Wing, which were built in the

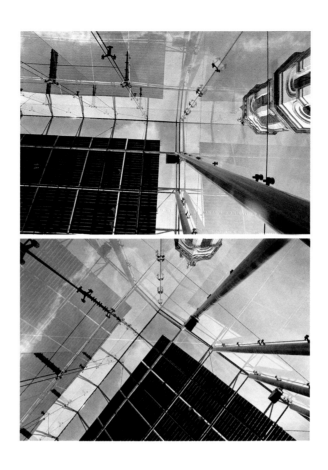

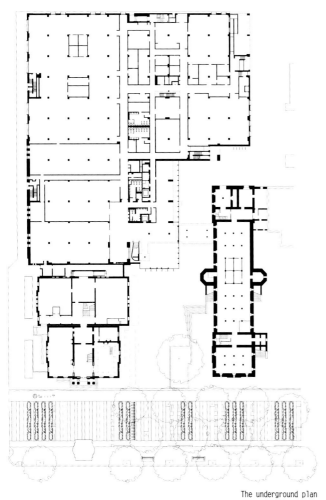

The underground plan

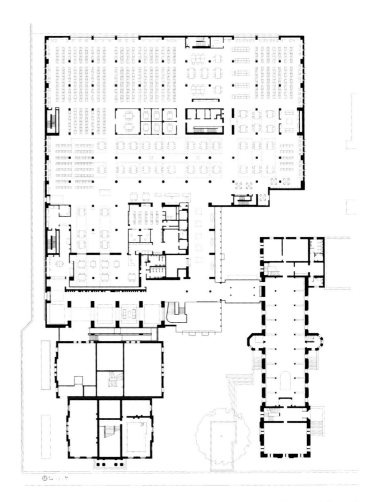

The ground floor plan

19th century, are renovated. Secondly, the wall and roof of the Spence Wing, which was built in the 1960s, were reconstructed, such that the users can enjoy the sunshine and, at the same time, enjoy the beautiful scenery outside. Lastly, through the renovation of the elements above, a new passage is constructed, which allows people to reach the core historical zone in the cultural zone. Cleaning the external materials of the building can ensure its long-lastingness; repairing the old materials or re-placing them with new ones can reconcile the entire construction effect. A sunlight control-ling device has been installed to the newly-opened windows, enriching the 3D effect of the streets.

It is hoped that the reconstruction project could help each building strike a balance among the groups of buildings, such that their original shape can still be seen, and that an open garden for the public can be composed. As a result, one can easily see the place from the northern terrance.

These two historical constructions of the 19th century define the boundary of east to west in the garden by colorful stone craft walls. A 15m high entrance of the bright hall is an extended part of the Spence Wing, which

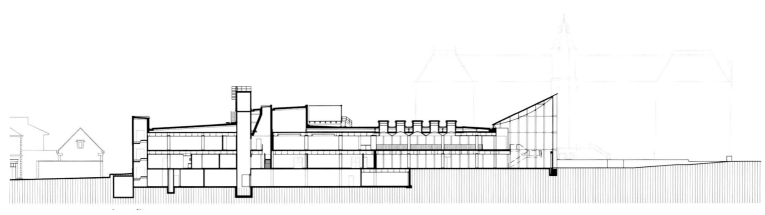

matches well with the old architecture and provides a sense of harmony. People can notice it whenever and wherever they are. The hall has brought the library a very important visual guidance. At daytime, the hall is filled with sunshine; during nighttime, it is also lighted by abundant lights. A highly efficient transparent glass film is inserted between the walls and roof. At the same time, in order to keep the building in a good condition, a metal sky-window Is hung and it creates an atmosphere which makes people feel like staying in the pavilion or the garden under a big tree.

The art project was planned and designed by MGT partner Pamille Berg. In the limited hall space, the artist Kay Lawrence created a set of relative plans and three-dimensional artworks. He explains the concepts of location, communication, information and community. In the seated area, along the "treasure wall", there are three big tailor-made tapestries which were designed by an artist, Pantjiti McKenzie, who is from a local community art center-Ernabella Arts Inc.

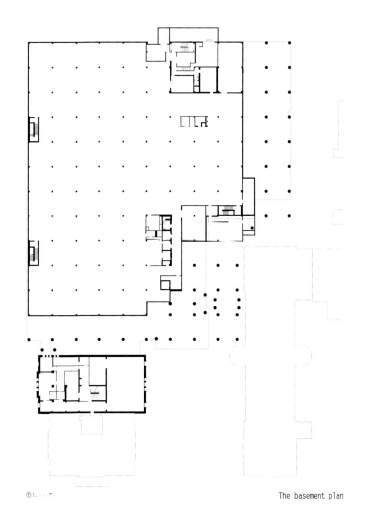

The basement plan

Clients   Government of Qatar
The main contractor   Hadi Simaan and Etienne Tricaud (AREP), architects
Architects   AREP (Bruno Sarret, Eric Dussiot, Marie–Odile Bosc, Ali Dehbonei, Alan Murray, Cyril Hugon, Ana Paula Vaz Correa, Stephane Mairesse)
Structure engineer   OVE ARUP
Construction company   Besix–Midmac
Photos   BESIX–AREP

The Doha Sports City Tower

The Doha Sports City Tower, part of the 2006 Asian Games conference, is a symbol construction of the entire sports center and the highest building in the city. The entire 130–hectared sports ground is viewable from the top tower. The design of the building is just as a bunch of burning torch because of the elegant parabola shape.

The design concept is built on the clear and organized structures of each component. The solid structure in the middle is supported by several bracket structures. These structures include hotel, president suite, sports museum, panorama restaurant, and the scenery terrace on the top. The highest level is constructed below the tower in which the Olympic flame is burning. People are not just able to see the huge screen surrounding the flame, but also a 360 degree urban scenery including the cities, sea and desert. Such majestic scenery makes people surprised.

The whole building was covered by frosted metal materials, and the sunny side is covered by frosted stainless steel which strengthens the surface of the lunate shape. In order to strengthen the wind resistant function, many holes are dug from the tower bottom to the top. The hall is the first part of the tower, and it includes a lobby on the first floor, the function room on the second floor and the restaurant on the third floor. The hotel has 7 floors for standard guest rooms and one floor for suites. A swimming pool and a gymnasium center are located at the air garden. One top floor of the hotel, there are also a sports museum, the president suite and the scenery terrace.

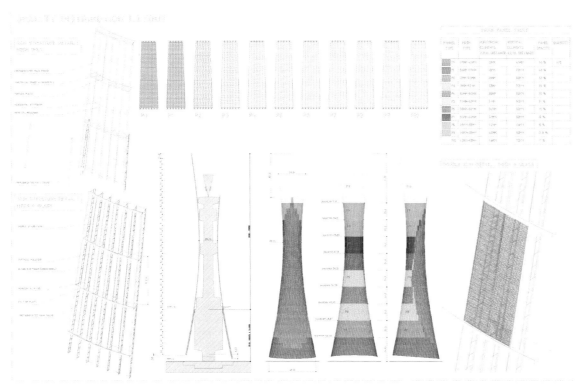

Material used from base to top

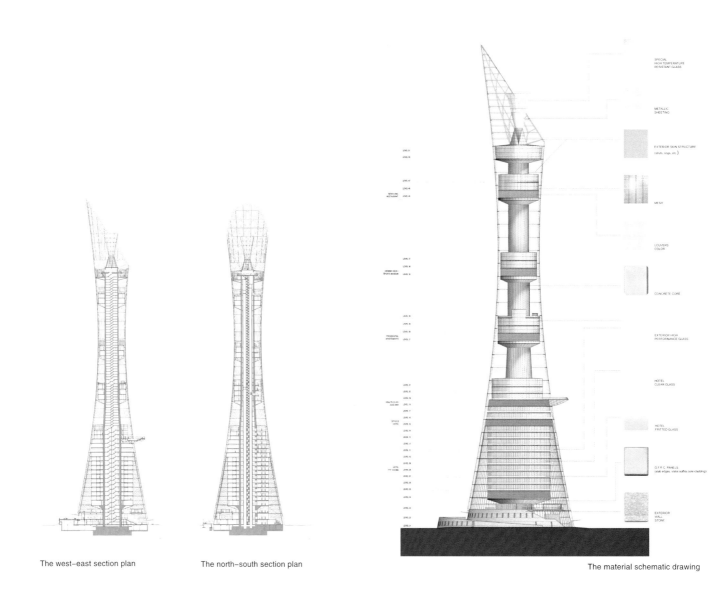

The west–east section plan

The north–south section plan

The material schematic drawing

The general layout

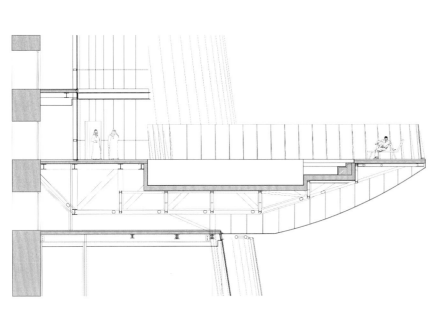

The swimming pool detail plan

The ground floor plan

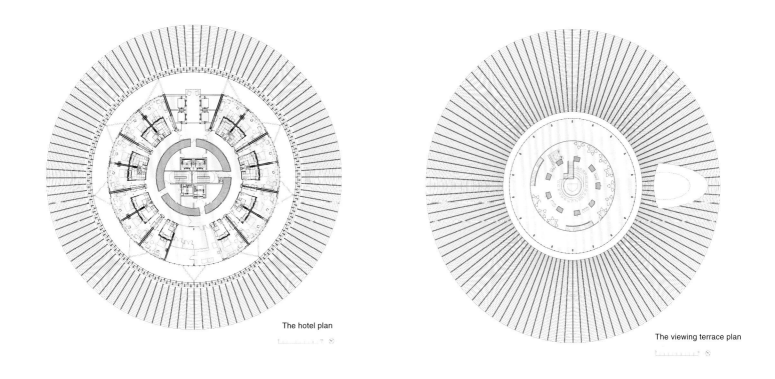

The hotel plan

The viewing terrace plan

Sports Hall TÜBINGEN

Location	Tübingen, Germany
Clients	Universitätsstadt Tübingen
Architect	Allmann Sattler Wappner Architekten GmbH
Partner	Markus Allmann, Dirk Bauer, Frank Kartheim, Olga Ritter, Alex Wagner
Project construction	Markus Allmann , Ludwig Wappner, Dirk Bauer, Birgit Bader, Eva Hartl, Kai Homm, Christof Kilius, Thomas Meusburger, Martin Plock, Ulf Rossler, Steffen Schwarz
Project management	Elwert & Stottele, Architektur-Projektmanagement
The structure engineer	Werner Sobek Ingenieure GmbH
Sources consultant	TransSolar Energietechnik GmbH
Engine & electric service	Interplan Gebaudetechnik GmbH
Construction physics	Horstmann + Berger
Fireproofing engineer	Kersken & Kirchner
Photos	Jens passoth
Construction area	6 500 m²
Cubage	40 700 m³
Used area	300 m²

In order to fulfill the design idea of the gymnasium, the indoor facilities can be used for professional sports items, so the Sports club, school games as well as other different types of fashionable sports can be here. All of these have been integrated subtly to satisfy the different requirements. At the same time, it brings beautiful scenery to the small town and aslo makes it a part of city facilities. A round green sport area is in the front. The entrance has been arranged on the first floor, near to the existing channel at the Northeast. There is a natural platform crossing the existing low-layer outdoor sports area.

The clear time-gap makes the "simultaneous sharing" become ture. It also makes the area of the sports hall able to be used repeatedly. With changing requirements, the spaces in the sport hall can be combined freely. Due to the difference in projects, the lower floors have been arranged with more than 3 000 seats. For some large-scale sports games, the trainning racetracks with telescopic platform can meet the audience's needs. Its appearance is also endowed with various functions, which can be a combined part of the sport hall. Hence, the hall becomes a new place to hold competitions of the Tübingen as wall as the center of fashionable sports.

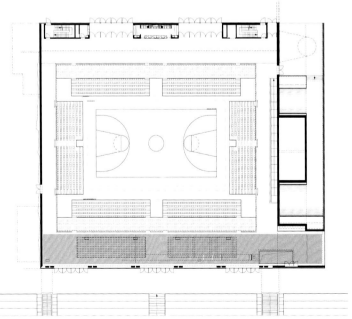

The ground floor plan

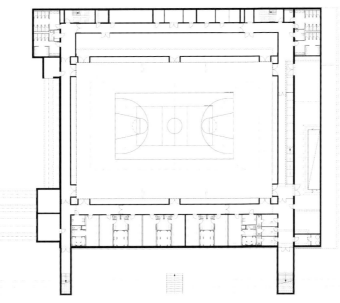

The first floor plan

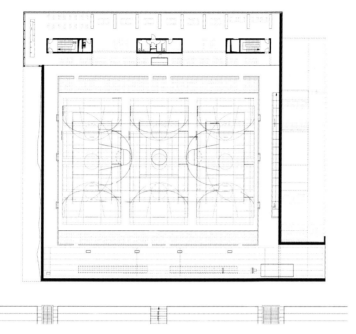

The plan

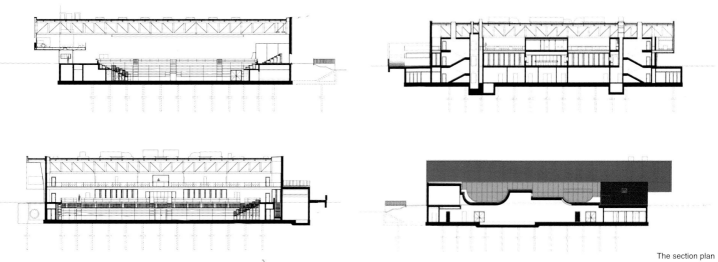

The section plan

Location   Kapyla Sport Park, Helsinki, Finland
Clients   City of Helsinki
Architect   Ajla Selenic Architecture & Design
The main designer   Ajla Selenic
Product designer   Anti Vuotilainen
Photos   Saku Paasilahti
Text   Ajla Selenic

Sport Pavilions in Helsinki, Finland

Helsinki City needs workable solutions to the construction of a series of sports centres, which include the dressing room for sports teams and coaches and a facility room for the maintenance of equipment. It aims to provide numerous sports centres to satisfy the public's needs. The function of this sports centre is to be a skating rink in winter and a tennis court in summer. Except strengthening the planning of its functions, another important need is to choose a kind of durable and fireproofing materials to construct the outer-walls.

Having considered the construction types and situations of the surrounding athletic fields, the architects have chosen a narrow linear plan to construct the building. People are able to see the field's activities from the indoor. A channel which separates the public area and the service area (including equipment room, working place and parking garage) connects the streets and the field and also provides an alternative way to enter the athletic field.

The concision of the linear plan promotes the architects' pursuit for a more expressive plan. And the style of building is developed towards a prefabricated structure. Through inserting waving patterns, the back elevation stretches into the roof gently, bringing a unique carven style to the construction and adds softness to the originally fierce wave-liked steel boards.

In order to express the lightness, the movement and the speed, the construction is built in the way of lift-off. The construction method is referred to the traditional Finland

SPORT PAVILION AND SERVICE BUILDING KAPYLA IN HELSINKI / SITE PLAN 1.1000

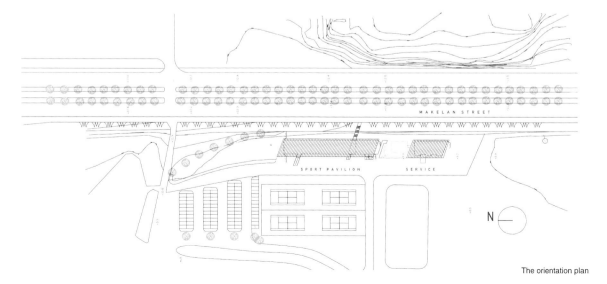

The orientation plan

original log cabin building—method which is also a solution to reducing the construction on the ground. Through the inclined path which is built on the lift level, the main entrance of the sports centre is emphasized. The load—bearing steel structure is prefab, and each group composed of 3 meters is used as a component and can be built quickly. For the construction, a double metal column system is applied in both the exterior and interior part, making the whole building light and elegant. The same design concept is also used in the inside, creating a sensation of lightness and liveliness. The design of the dressing room is simple and linear, and the main color combination is gray, white and yellow. Warm yellow has also been used in the indoor to compel against the cool metal feeling and replace the sunlight and warmth which can hardly be found at the north. Passion is also stimulated even in the dark winter.

In 2001, Ajla Selenic, a Serbian architect in Finland, won the Annual Award for Architecture in Serbia by this project.

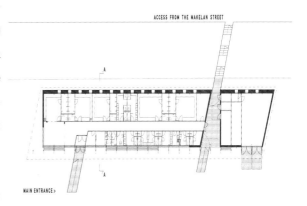

The plan

SPORT PAVILION KAPYLA IN HELSINKI / NORTH ELEVATION 1:1 0 0

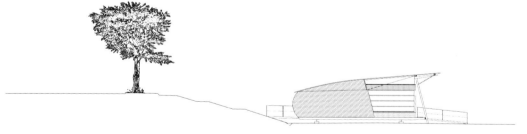

The north elevation

SPORT PAVILION KAPYLA IN HELSINKI / SECTION 1:100

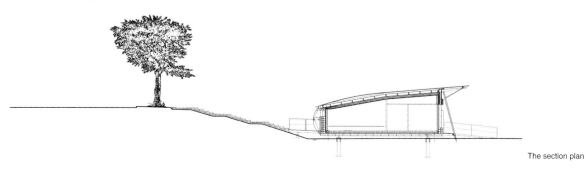

The section plan

SPORT PAVILION IN KAPYLA HELSINKI / WEST ELEVATION 1:200

The west elevation plan

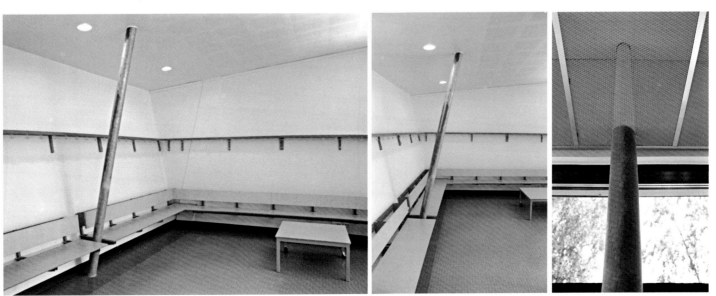

Location Alphen aan den Rijn, The Netherlands
Architect Kraaijvanger Urbis
Photos Jeroen Musch

Theatre and Cinema Castellum

The project is a core part of the city center development plan of Castellum. The most noticeable part is the central plaza located at the Rhine bank. One of the major targets of this project is to locate this public building in a suitable place. Many shops, bars and restaurants can be found in the plaza. Thus, extra efforts should be made to ensure the informal settings in the area matches with the name of "home of the culture" of the place.

Compared with the building area, the scale of whole project is really huge. Planning the design is like solving a crossword puzzle. The whole project includes a main theatre that comprises 749 seats, a multi-purpose hall with 240 seats and a cinema which has 3 showing halls.

The main theatre and the entrance hall are designed together to match with the design of the stage staves. The outer layer of the construction is made of a wave-shaped aluminum board and is named "the storm of desert".

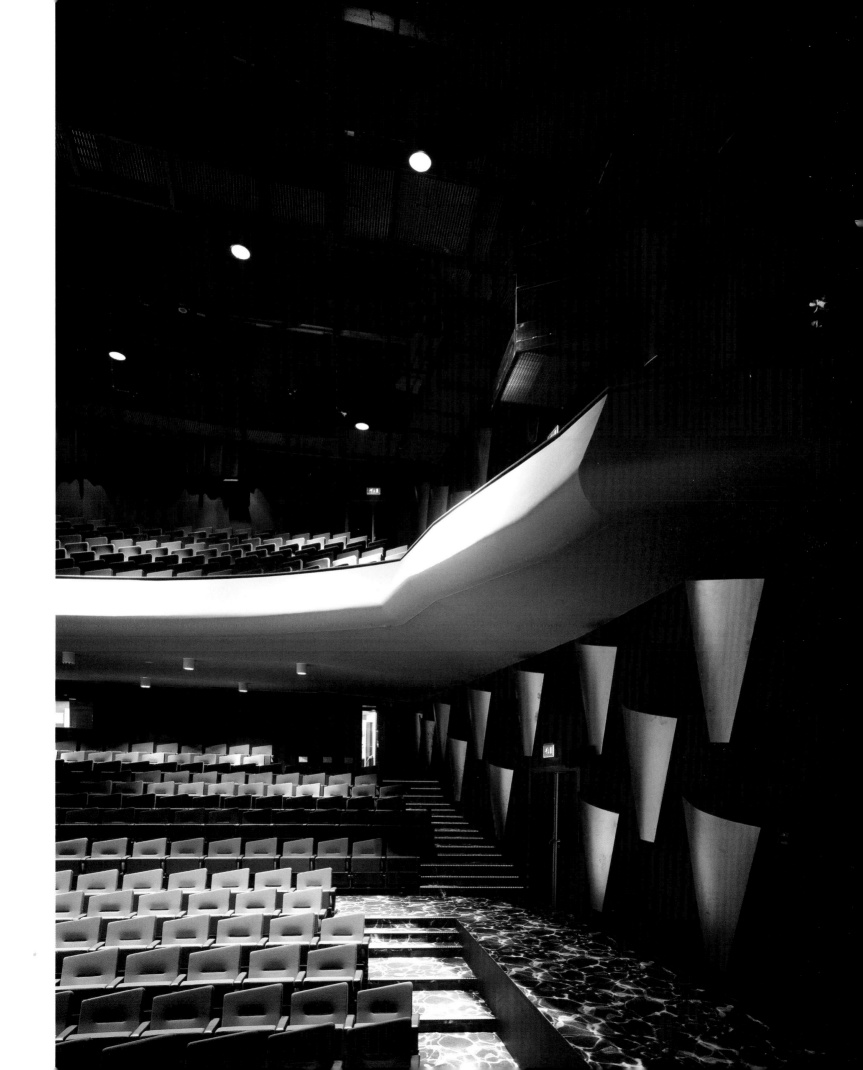

Location   Amsterdam, The Netherlands

Clients   Gemeente Amsterdam

The area   18 000 m²

Architects   3XN Kim Herforth Nielsen, Bo Boje Larsen, Kim Christiansen

The design team   Palle Holsting, Rasmus Holm, Torbenastergaard, Ole astergaard, Uffe Bay-Schmidt, Flemming Christiansen,

Engineer   Eva Hard ABT BV, The Netherlands

Contractor   BAM BV, The Netherlands

Completed   2005

Photos   Adam Mark

The plan   Courtesy 3XNielsen

Centre for Modern Music, Amsterdam

"BIMhuis" Modern Music Center, which was designed by 3Xnielsen Architect office, won the first grade in the International Architectural Design Competition. The competition was held in 1997 in Amsterdam newly designed Music Center. Although the music hall is located at a side of Fjord river wharf, it is still closely connected with the Amsterdam, a canal city.

The design plan for the music hall has two parts. The first part is a square base composed by two musical boxes and a big group of staircase. The second part includes the concert hall, BIMhuis, which is hung above the square base and plays Jazz and impromptu music. It also includes the modern music concert hall—the Ijsbreker, which is built on the group of staircase.

The BIMhuis has about 300 seats. However, the Ijsbreker can provide about 800 seats. Those diversified construction elements have been unified together under the roof which has just one floor. When people view the CMM far away, it resembles a huge city symbol construction which is built near the river. When you observe it by a short distance, you will find that the center could be divided into several kinds of elements. This is the purpose of architects—to creat a modern garden in city such that everyone is able to enjoy a wonderful time there.

The BIMhuis modern music center is a construction which uses music as the main theme. It integrates two kinds of historical culture facilities—the Ijsbreker morden music concert hall and The BIMhuis Jazz and impromptu music hall. Although the center is built

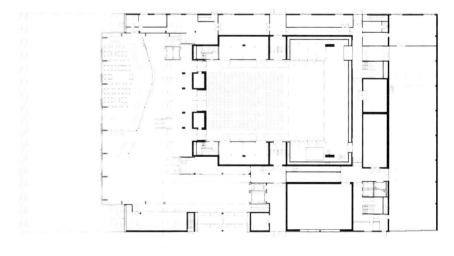

The ground floor plan

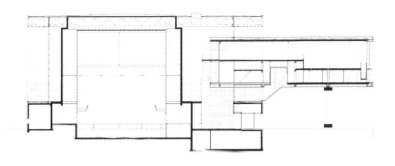

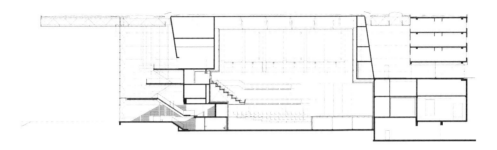

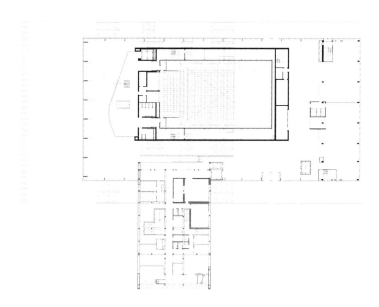

The first floor plan

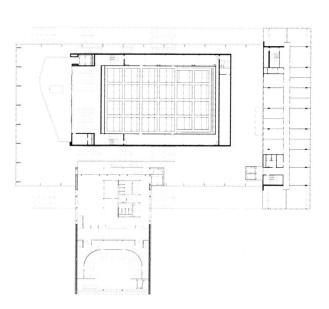

The second floor plan

on the Heinkade wharf, it is still connected closely with the inner part of the Channel city .The main concept of design is to create an interesting public place in the newly developed area of Amsterdam city.

The position and the layout of the center are the master-piece of the designers .The center has 5 equally important outer-wall elevations, two of which face the river and one faces the urban area and the Zouthaven reservoir which is under construction.

In order to bulid a truly "public" construction, designers have designed a footpath which is open for 24 hours. In spite of the kind of program being played in the BIMhuis or the Ijsbreker, the footpath will be open for the pubilc. It passes trhough the broad stairs and becoms a connection part between the center, the wharf, and the water surface. It also becoms an attractive path which is attached to the center interior.

Location   Detroit, Michigan, USA
Clients   Detroit Symphony Orchestra
Architects Diamond and Schmitt Architects Inc.
Photos   Steven Evans

Detroit Symphony Orchestra

The 1919 symphony hall of one of the most attractive cultural organizations in USA—Detroit Symphony Orchestra (Hereafter referred to as DSO) was designed by Raymond Crane. The sound effects are widely appreciated, yet the total area is only 4 830sqm. DSO found the area of the Symphony hall too small to meet the needs. A large space is needed at the backstage for rehearsal and training, so that a larger multi—functional public area could be provided to the customers. The Diamond and Schmitt Architects was invited to take charge of the rebuilding and redesigning for expansion of the project. It is planned to invest 60 000 000 US dollars to rebuild it and meet the abovementioned growing needs. A new gathering place has been built to provide accessorial facilities and music education facilities for actors; a brand new theater named "music box", which comprises 450 seats, is also added. The whole newly built part is named as "Max M.Ficsher" music center, which symbolizes the Symphony Orchestra as well as the renaissance of its "family" town—Midtown.

In the newly built part, the most noticeable section is the four—floor high atrium great hall, which comprises bars, leisure seated area, indoor gallery and, most importantly, the grandest and most sparkling staircase, which is the shiniest point of this great hall. The whole of the hall covers about 1 580sqm, 3 times larger than the original one. Architects have used various kinds of materials such as bronze, stone glass, steel, etc. to create a sharp industrial image in the hall whilst keeping a warm and passionate sensation at the same time. Architects made use of such details ingeniously to express respect to Detroit,

the historic "manufacture town". The design very much matches with the other parts of this project; it also becomes the most important part of the renewal project of the existing historic Symphony Orchestra. The Symphony Orchestra has already been recorded at the American national scenic spot and historic resort registry.

The newly-added facilities have enormously improved the quality and flexibility of the existing accessorial, training and administrative division of the DSO. The new facilities include a 2 136sqm musician dress room and musical instrument storage as well as a 1 115sqm administrative office. A new music training center, which covers 929sqm has become a training area and it includes training room, technology center, music library and a rehearsal hall for DOS young musicians. The "Music Box" has occupied a large portion of the total area of this project. It has added much flexibility to the DOS music program arrangement. Through an adjustable symphony

The east elevation plan

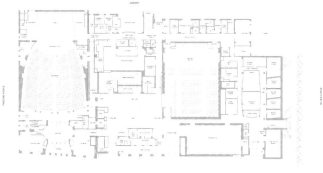

The ground floor plan

system, the hall is now able to produce the best sound effect to match with the large variety of music, including jazz, classical and popular music. In additional, it provides an alternative place to the main performing hall, so that DSO and other music companies can perform different types of music. It also allows two performances to take place simultaneously in the two performing halls. The construction of a wider place for storage, training, dressing, and even the new theatre is a result of DSO staff's continuous and widespread consultation.

Besides the renovation of the surface of the existing building, the expansion project also added a new building to the original one, which connects to the street. Although basic geometrical shapes, which have appeared on the DSO, are used repeatedly, it also reapplies the neoclassicism construction technique in a humorous way, and furnish this building, which was built in 1919, with brand new features. The Corinthian pillar of Raymond Crane's style has been turned to an extrusive vertical blue copper belt. It is used to separate the smooth glasses from the three floors. On the first floor, there are 5 transparent entrances which reflect the indoor activities to the sidewalk outside. It also makes the Detroit central area's vista become exceptionally lively. A brand new musical instrument store, which is open at the same level, brings a lot of amusement to the floors close to the street.

All in all, the new facilities are named as "the Max" by the Detroit people. It is brand new. Specifically, it does not only signify the reborn of the famous Symphony Orchestra, but also the support for Symphony Orchestra's development and the city's renovation. This way, the vigor of Detroit Symphony Orchestra can last forever.

The first floor plan

Location Toronto, Ontario, Canada
Clients University of Toronto, Canada
Architects Behnisch Architekten, with architectsAlliance, Toronto
Photos Martin Werminghausen, David Cook, Tom Arban
Completed 2005
Total area 20 630 m²

Terrence Donnelly Centre for Cellular and Biomolecular Research at the University of Toronto

The University of Toronto together with the affiliated organization is an outstanding institution which seeks and researches on the relationship between gene and disease. The Terrence Donnelly Center for Cellular and Biomolecular Research (hereafter referred to as 'CCBR') will provide the top laboratory and facilities for this university and brings advantages to the biological molecule research. The design proposal sparkplugs a kind of interdisciplinary CCBR concept, which invites 400 experts who come from different research aspects, including computer scientists, physicists, pharmacists and engineers. At the same time, an interaction among them can take place, realizing the flexibility and technological advancement within the facilities.

The construction is built in the centre of the university area, at the Circular Square and Empress Park in King's College. It creates a brand new appearance of the university which is on the busy city street. In the external and internal working environment, it not only reflects the university's status in genetic research, but also eliminates the gulf be—tween the historical characteristics of the construction and the top technical status of CCBR, integrating the two perfectly.

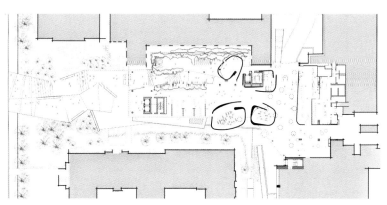

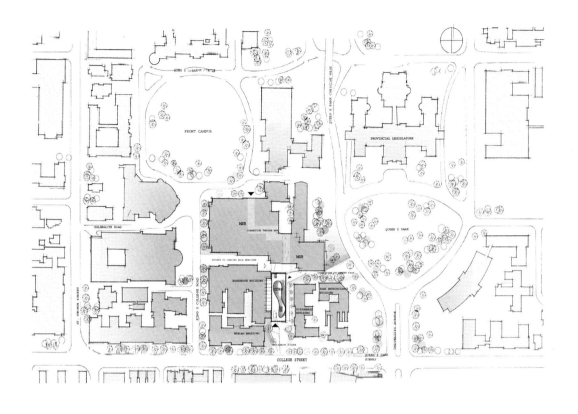

This project is a 12-storey square transparent construction which is built on a public square. In the square, there are the offices, seminar facilities and dining room for teaching and administrative staff. Its style is totally different with the square-shaped glass building and thus a sharp contrast is formed. The architects made use of the limited area and built a new public forum for the university. After being renovated, the scenery of the garden plays an important role in preserving the existing public passages. The square roof panel forms a giant atrium. The garden which has two or three floors shows the setting and characteristics of the building, forming a rarely found independent workplace. The whole building makes full use of sunlight, and has also achieved the goal of having natural ventilation. Therefore, the outer elevation has a unique style which is not gloomy nor dazzling.

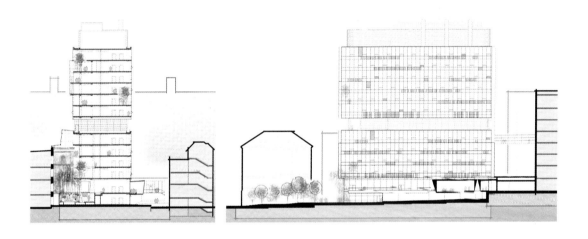

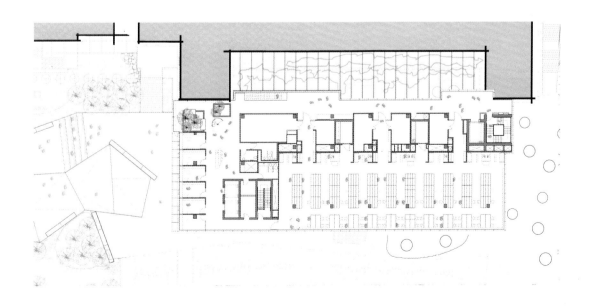

Location   Cambridge, MA, USA

Clients   Genzyme Corporation and Lyme
Properties, US

Architects& Collectivity layout   Behnisch, Behnisch&Partner, Inc., US;
tenent improvement by Next Phase
Studios, US

Surroundings & Structure consultant   Buro Happold, UK and US

The main contractor   Turner Construction

The area   32 515 m²

Genzyme Center

The Genzyme Center is an office building that is able to accommodate 920 people. There are also set stores, restaurants and the ground floor public zone. It is developed and built by a private developer who is specialized in doing laboratory building with some famous biology science & technology companies. Amidst so many research offices, the office building stands as an unique mark, which symbolizes advancement, the design of it integrates practicality and diversity into the whole building and the nature environment.

The glass shell, unadorned but with the remarkable performance, unifies the city to go fight against the bad weather in Boston and also prevent the exterior climate from influencing the interior design. Seen from the street, the light and transparent glass elevation draws out the appearance of the construction, which has colorful windows and curtains, and the silk-screen pictures on the the window blinds and the back of glass, adding more interests and colors to it. An outdoor garden strengthens the depth and transparency and reflection the elevation, and making its image changable every time.

The lower layer has a public area, which supplies a brand-new activity place to neighbors. Before reaching the interlayer's reception, the visitors and the staff have to

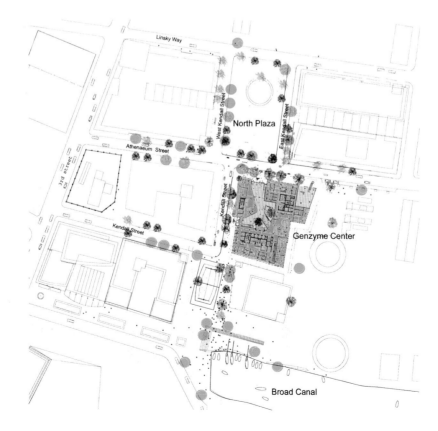

The general layout

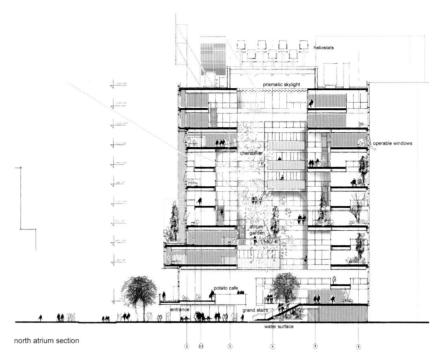

north atrium section

The north atrium section plan

pass a beautiful garden, which is filled with green trees and running water. The Offices above the public area is in open style. So it brings convenience to other various space layouts.

The 12-floor atrium as a climate oasis, just like a big tree stretching out so many branches, extends from the center to the surface and forms a special connection interlacing each other. The atrium connects each working place, the public area and the garden, and it looks like a vertical city. There are various office landscapes: the open working place and the closed office interweave each other. The landscape varies according to different requirements and locations. A private-gathering working place has been set opposite to such public spaces subtly, for example, the garden and the atrium.

The window blinds refracts the sunshine to supply natural light for most offices. However, the atrium depends on various facilities to get natural lighting. The prism-ceiling under the skylight leaches the sunlight to reduce giddy effects and also keep suitable brightness. The leached-sunlight is reflected by man-made chandeliers and the "light wall" everywhere. The chandeliers are made of acryl prism, so the reflected rainbow-light and the changing patterns from it make the whole atrium vivid and changing following the sunlight. Otherwise, The exposal-directional system (the heliostat with fixed mirror) strengthens the lighting of the atrium.

Genzyme Center construction shell adopted excellent glass system, and the 12 floors are equipped with such windows, which could be controlled by switchs.

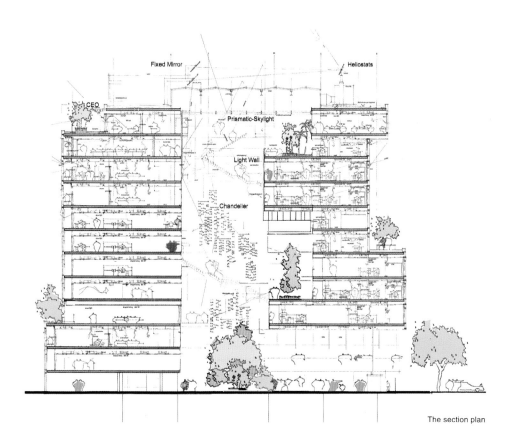

The section plan

The 13th floor plan

The 6th floor plan

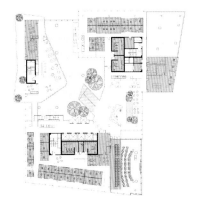

The 3th floor plan

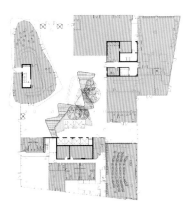

The ground floor plan

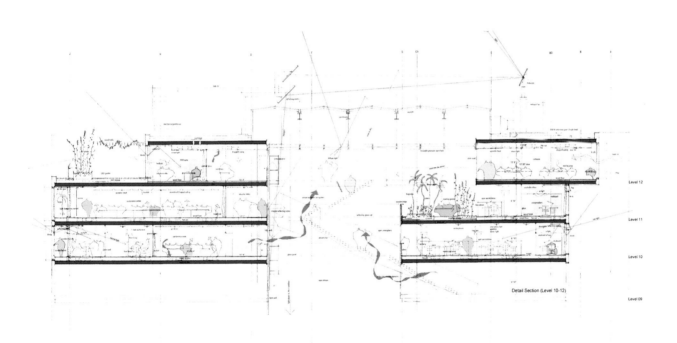

Detail Section (Level 10-12)

Level 12

Level 11

Level 10

Level 09

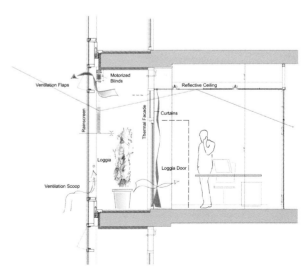

Ventilation Flaps

Motorized Blinds

Reflective Ceiling

Rainscreen

Thermal Facade

Curtains

Loggia

Loggia Door

Ventilation Scoop

Location   Amsterdam, Netherlands
Architects   Rafael Vinoly Architects
Photos   Raoul Suermondt
Plan and effect drawing   Courtesy of Rafael Vinoly Architects
The total area   9 832 m²
Completed   2005

Mahler 4 Office Tower

The project is located at the south heartland of Amsterdam. It is a multi–functional development zone, which covers 160 000sqm in total. It is designed by the Rafael Vinoly Architects together with other 8 architects who also contributed to making an overall plan for this piece of land and established a designing standard to guarantee the uniformity throughout the project.

The overall plan has completely abandoned the traditional urban design planning, which is controlled by the principle of having equal amount of materials and same designing connotation. The new design enriches the surrounding environment and integrates such environment with this historical city. All of these plans use two strategies towards changing the rituals: 1) to define the basic spatial structure of void space and then outline the development zone through reduction of void space; 2) to avoid using the base, column, roof structure of traditional skyscrapers' design, and replace it with multi–layer construction order which is totally different from the former, strengthening the thought of perceiving a city from various levels and aspects.

The proposal is to reinterpret the two–dimensional data as a more dynamic geometric solid, which outlines the fire evacuation plan surrounding the outside of the building and forms a more complete proposal. The building's surface is composed of vertical solid frames, so it makes the huge building unified and brings different characteristics to each dimension. The open staircase provides a possibility for the users to make use of the exterior space, which can be used as gardens and places for outdoor activities on each floor. The design of the whole building is like the creation of a sculpture. It is not merely a design on the surface.

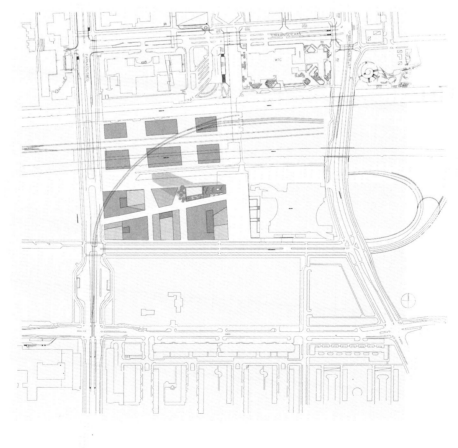

The orientation plan

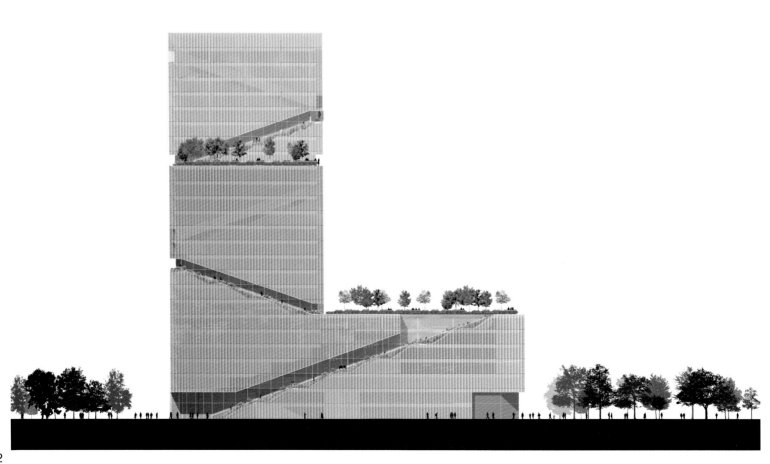

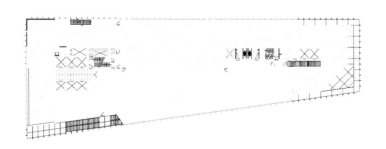

The middle floor plan

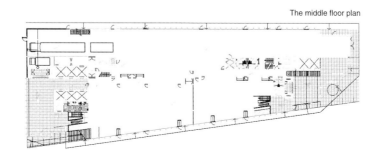

Location   Copenhagen, Denmark.
Clients   FIH A/S
The area   12 000 m²
Architect   3XNielsen (Kim Herforth Nielsen, Kim Christiansen, Bo Boje
                Larsen)
3XN design team Kim Herforth Nielsen, Anne Mikkelsen, Rasmus Holm, Mikkel
                Schlesinger, Carsten Olsen, Henning
                Moeskjaer, Olav Norgaard, Mark Hoffmann-Holst
Landscape design Jeppe Aagaard Andersen
Contractor   NCC
Engineer   COWI, HAMI Consult
Photos   Adam Mark

FIH Domicile, Copenhagen

The Headquarters of The FIH Denmark Industrial investment Bank has moved into the new address Langelinie in May 2002. The client wanted the building to be designed by simple, intense, high-expressive lines and at the same time, endowed with various meanings, and able to meet the architectural style of the nearby area, the Dahlerups Pakhus which was once used as storage. It is required by this area that the planning and construction of Langelinie pier should match with Dahlerup Pakhus in the aspects of volume and materials chosen.

The surface area of FIH building is the same as the Dahlerups Pakhus', but the difference is that the new headquarter building is a light, transparent modern architecture which is open to the nearby scenery. The surface covered by red brown bricks is just like Dahlerups Pakhus' but the difference is the brick covered in FIH is a kind of brick-broad which is hung on the surface.

Semblance: An appliance

The surface of FIH building construction is not as thick as the Dahlerups Pakhus's. It is because the building contains a long slit which adjusts its size according to the weather. From the natural perspective, it is more like equipment or even a kind of machine. The architecture's surface is composed of three kinds of materials, and each of them is as tall as one floor. The layer in between is a glass board, whose inside are some red-brown

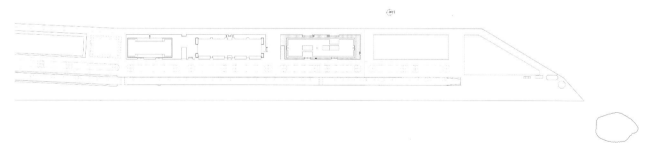

The orientation plan

The ground floor plan

The second floor plan

brick boards, which are of the same height and quantity. The outside is covered by alum-Persian blinds which are fixed by the horizontal frames, together with adjustable metal window blind strips slipping freely in the same direction. The size of Persian blinds match with the glass boards and bricks inside. It slides right in front of those boards. The sliding is adjusted by the sensitimeter automatically. When it receives direct sunshine, the Persian-blinds will slide to the window and block the sunlight, creating a horizontal view. And when there is a lack of sunlight, the Persian-blinds will move away from the windows automatically and stay at the front of the brick boards. It creates two totally different appearances, namely aluminum alloy with windows or with bricks. The Persian-blinds can also be controlled by people, showing the flexibility. When the blinds are closed, fresh air can still penetrate the windows, providing natural ventilation.

The Whole: Transparent "hanging garden"

The 25m-deep construction is quite suitable to be a storage yet it is not the best choice for office building. This poses a tremendous challenge to the construction-how to allow light and air in the construction.

The landscape designer Jeppe Aagaard Andersen carved and dug two gigantic deep notches in the headquarter building, in order to let sunlight come into the building. It also

becomes an entrance and a leisure garden for visitors. The notches inside are connected with the axis line and extend upward to several floors. They all have their own heights matching with one another. The visitors go upstairs from the lobby stairs or the glass elevator, then they will be able to see two hanging gardens: the eastern Trekroner Fort and the western Midtermolen Wharf.

The building office is composed of half-open office zones and independent office units. People can enjoy the beautiful scenery: both the landscape outside and the garden inside through the transparent glass windows. Fresh air and fine ventilation can be enjoyed.

Light design

3Xnielsen cooperated with Steven Scott, who is a light artist and stage designer, whose light works can be integrated into architectures completely. Using 3 kinds of fluorescent lamps as base which have its own basic color just as the principle of television screen, the designer created two special optics art works hanging in the lobby beside the two elevators. The colour of the work changes automatically by the preinstall system. A cycle amounts to 60 seconds. The colour change matches with the elevator. When the elevator starts working, artwork is also driven to change its colour.

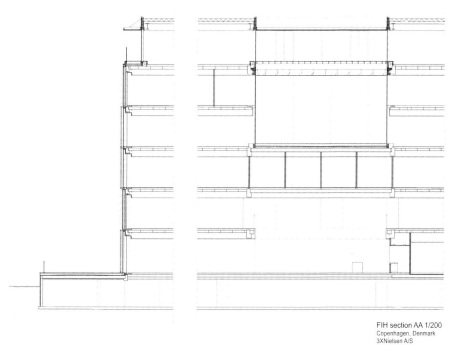

FIH section AA 1/200
Copenhagen, Denmark
3XNielsen A/S   The section plan A

FIH ETAGE04_3 SAL 1/400

The third floor plan

FIH ETAGE06 - 5 SAL 1/400

The fifth floor plan

The section plan B

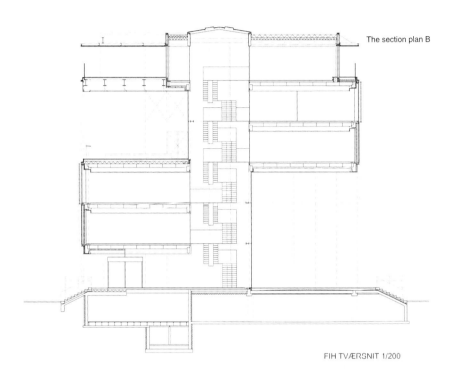

FIH TVÆRSNIT 1/200

TOD'S Tokyo Building

The TOD's Tokyo building is the masterpiece of Toyo Ito which has been constructed for several years. The building faces the Tokyo street and has 7 floors, with the total area of around 2 550sqm. The TOD's retail stores inside are arranged on the first and second floors. Part of the third floor as well as the fourth and fifth floors are used as offices. A function room can be found on the sixth floor. Private meeting room and garden are arranged on the top floor.

Toyo Ito said, "TOD's Tokyo building is an architectural project full of ambition; it manifests the epoch–making construction concept and technology completely. I would like to make a breakthrough to the modern architectural style of the 20th Century this project."

The architect adopts six surfaces to compose an "L" pattern in the building, and the most unique part is the front face design, which creates an imagination of a group of elms. This complex shape is constructed by a concrete building. The designer adds a piece of glass in each channel, making the design like 9 contraposed trees. There is no frame in between the concrete and glass such that the liveliness and the characteristics of the materials could be brought out through idiographic parataxis effects. This concrete building was built by using advanced structural analysis and construction technique. When compared with other architectures with traditional glass faces on the Tokoy Street, its design is very special and appealing.

The total area of the first and second floors as well as part of the third floor is about

600sqm. The entrance gate was built of glass screen which is cut as crystal and can be used as showing windows. The building gathers sunlight from different directions, patching up with the interior materials (such as wood and furs) and creating an elegant space. Moving upwards along the natural tree-shaped structure, the environment at higher elevation is much different with that below. The overlapping "branches" creates a comfortable sensation for the office floors, the splendid activity space and the roof garden. The tree-shaped structure also create a beautiful space. The environmental atmosphere changes as we move upwards, showing a unique concept of design.

Toyo Ito have had several experimental architectural projects in the past and obtained great results. His works include the Sendai Media Center, The Brugge Exhibition Hall in 2002, the London Serpentine Exhibition Hall and so on.

Location   Copenhagen, Denmark
The area   9.550 m² (expect basement)
Clients   Sampension A/S
Architects   3XNielsen (Kim Herforth Nielsen, Kim Christiansen and
                   Bo Boje Larsen)

3XNielsen design team

Kim Herforth Nielsen, Anne Mikkelsen, Mikkel
Schlesinger, Lars Kjemtrup.Morten Kramer, Lars
Povlsen, Carsten Olsen, Anders Barslund, Gitte
Ingemann

Engineer   Ramball
Contractor   NCC
Photos   Adam Mark

Head Office of Sampension

The head office of Sampension, located at the newly established city, Tuborg Syd in Copenhagen. It is connected with the Sound, and is composed by 2 elements: a vertical stretched "L" corner and a horizontal square barrel. Both are on top of the building and are linked to the conical space in which the illuminating system is installed.

The surface of the "L" side of this building is covered by a kind of gray–green marble. In the barrel part there installed a layer of copper frame which turns from black to marble-green as time passes by. The copper surface resembles a stackable "CD box" which is as high as one floor. The directions to which these "CD Boxes" face are not unchangeable, with one facing outward and another facing inward. They are installed on the building surface alternately. This unique decorating technique creates an extrusive basso–relievo effect on the surface. For the glass part, the "CD Box" copper layer is designed as window blinds on which holes are drilled, so the blinds can turn around vertically. Then, these blinds can still block the sunlight from the east and west even in the winter, without blocking the beautiful scenery outside.

There is a circular revolving door fixed at the entrance of the building. And the door is positioned at a very special place–it is not placed in the front centre of the building, but on a glass screen which is at a corner far away from the building centre. The designer created a lovely and friendly atmosphere in this lobby which is one floor high. A solid

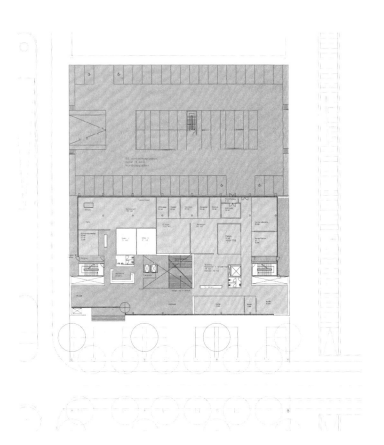

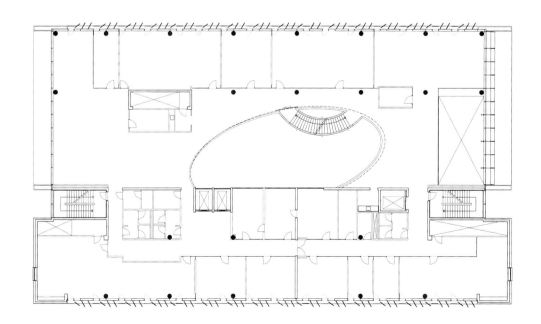

marble staircase enables people to go straight up to the atrium on the second floor. The ellipse-shaped atrium extends to the sharp angle part of the building. And at the same time, the atrium extends upwards and goes through all levels of the building. The facilities on the first floor include a restaurant, a meeting center and a series of small meeting rooms, with a passage leading to the terrace of the building's sharp angle. Light colors are used as the main color tone, creating a bright and subtle feeling for the whole building.

The water curtain art ware which is made of the optical fiber contains several functions. First, it hoists a transparent gauze curtain between the conference room and the quadrangle. Second, the water curtain optical fiber is changes the color slowly with the lapse of time. Third, the running water flows into the basin in the hall according to the textile, agglomerating massive water vapor in the hall. Such water vapor is helpful in improving the indoor humidity. Finally, the 'ding-dong' sound created the running water is able to reduce the noises from the surroundings, hence the noises created by the restaurant will not seem to be too grating.

Office Building Südwestmetall Reutlingen

Clients	Südwestmetall, Verband der Metall-und Elektroindustrie Baden-Württemberg e.V.
Architects	Allmann Sattler Wappner Architekten BDA
Project principal	Helgo von Meier
Design team	Georg Rafailidis, Angela Hertel, Bettina Mutzenbach, Susanne Rath
Conceptual & Armor plate	Roswitha Allmann Mediendesign
Landscape architect	Realgrun Landschaftsarchitekten
Project engineer	Saadma PAS Ingenieurburo VDI
Structure engineer	Sobek Ingenieure GmbH, Albstr
Sources engineer	TransSolar Energietechnik GmbH
Service engineer	Service Engineers Schreiber Beratende Ingenieure
Elevation engineer	Fuchs R+R, Ingenieurboro
Construction physics	Horstmann+Berger Ingenieurboro
Engine & electric engineer	Electrical Engineer Ingenieurboro Schwarz
Photos	Florian Holzherr, Jens Passoth
The plan	Allmann Sattler Wappner Architekten BDA
The area	4 200 m²
Cubage	16 200 m³

The building is the trainning center and office building of Sü-dwestmetall, which is a metal work and electric processing company of Baden-Württemberg in Germany. The constructions there are mostly old and half-wooden; and the walls are either made of mortar or of naked brick structure.

Onc of the typical characteristics of the building design is the saddleback roofs and the 15m-high front doors. In this area, the mixed use of housing, office, small factory is the most popular practice, which combines the characteristic of city-layout and the metal and electric power production.

Three buildings of saddleback roofs are suitable for the environment in both their mass and outer appearance, for instance, the height of ear-eaves, the shape of roof, the width of elevation, the depth of building, the trees and so on. A multi-funtional space separates the construction and each part has its own use. For example, the corner of Bismarckstrass and Schulstrasse is the public entrance of Südwestmetall. At the back of monomer construction, there is a garth, which is used as a personal terrace. The metal grill details for decoration are built from the ground and are 3m higher than the walls. The transparent parts separate the public area and the individual area. The grills are sur-rounded by trees creating a garden that connects the open area of the treetop and the first floor of the public space. The facade of the building is made of stainless board. The sunshade of the elevation is movable, which will be opened in daytime and closed in the evening and holidays.

The facade of the construction is between the central controlled sunshade and the independent sunlight adjuster, and has clear layers. Out of the concept of city layout, from streets to the construction facade, metal elements are used. The space is surrounded by metal grills, which people could touch from the outside. The 3m-high platform is divided by the metal grills, strengthening the visual feeling of stainless elevations. The ground floor includes all kinds of public functional areas, for example, the entrance, the reception room, the underground parking garage ramps and so on. Each room on the ground floor is capacious and does not have any column, so the whole elevation is transparent and luminous. The designing concept is flexible and practicable. Each grilled unit is not only designed as small independent offices, but also as open offices. In the square plane, an atrium is arranged to be a public area, which connects with another new area containing kitchen and toilet. It is an activify place for the staff. The training room and the meeting room are set on the second floor and both of them have their own characteristic. The loft's height is 9.6 meters and the sound box and the lights are set above the conference desk.

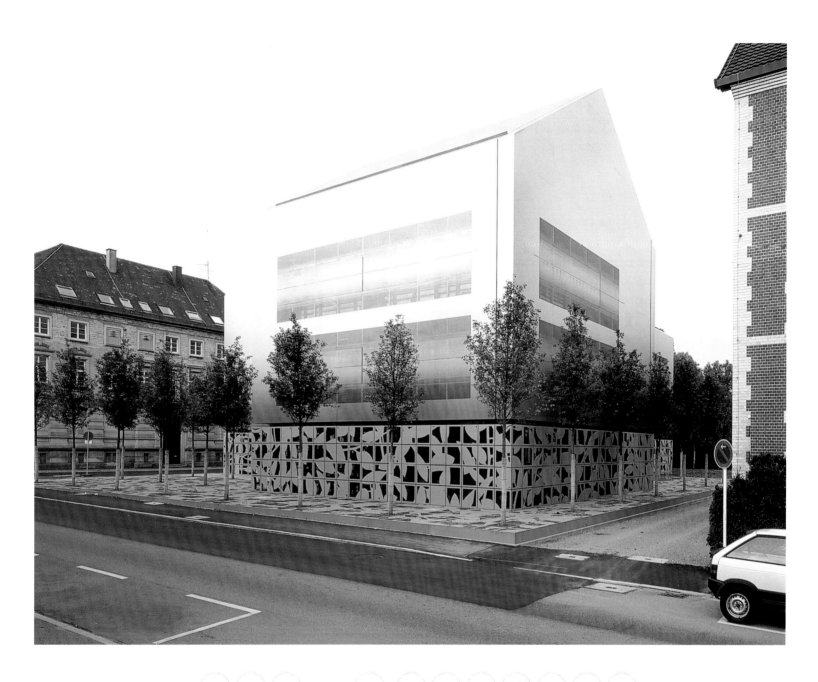

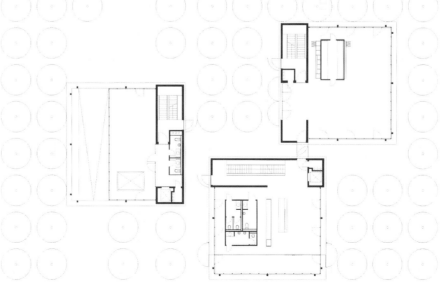

The plan

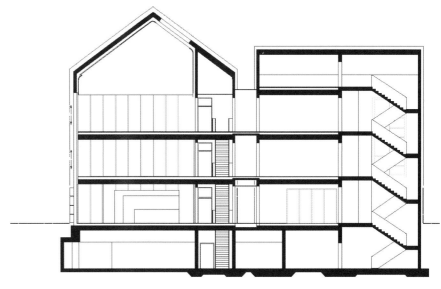

The section plan

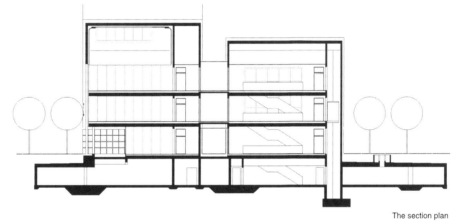

The section plan

Location Randers, Denmark
Clients Sparekassen Kronjylland
The area 7 600 m²
Architects 3XNielsen (Kim Herforth Nielsen, Kim Christiansen, Bo Boje Larsen)
3XN design team Kim Herforth Nielsen, Mette Dalsgaard, Tommy Bruun, Lars Povlsen, Holger Mouritzen, Klaus Petersen, Poul K. Jørgensen, Lars Due Jensen, Gerti Axelsen, Anders B. Christensen, Rikke Zachariasen, Pia Hallstrup
Landscape designer Kristine Jensen
Engineer Rambøll
Contractor NCC Denmark
Metope artwork Jens Bjerre
Photos Adam Mørk, Har Lyset
Plan and effect drawing Courtesy 3XN

Savings Bank Kronjylland Headquarters, Denmark

The Savings Bank Kronjylland's headquarters building is located at Gudena river shore in the Randers city. The new office building in the headquarters, which is on the bank green lawn, looks like an IC which has edges and corners. It becomes the unique geographical sign in the Randers city landscape. This bank headquarters, as the first building in this broad river bank lawn, has a great construction planning goal. It has also been awarded as "the natural scenery park which owns the monomer building groups."

The building is composed of 3 architectural elements such as a square base, a glass quartz spheroid and a wooden "box". The square base which is covered by black natural stones clearly divides the construction space. At the first floor, there are some transparent concaved screen walls which almost cannot be seen on the four walls. The screen wall subtly creates a kind of visual imagination—when people inside look upwards, they can see the glass quartz spheroid which occupies 3 floors, seemingly floating at the bottom of the black square. Several facilities are installed at the first floor, for instance, reception and other visitor-receiving facilities as well as the dining room.

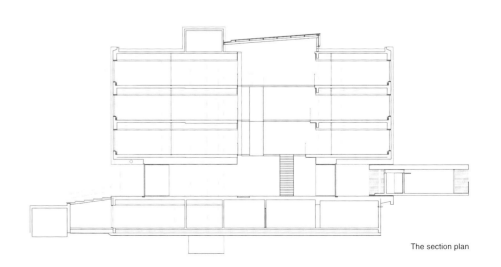

The section plan

The glass quartz spheroid part, which occupies 3 floors, comprises offices that are at the back of the external elevation. Inside the spheroid, there is an atrium which is connected with 3 floors, and on the top of it is a huge glass roof. A piece of vertical board surrounds the other rooms. An artwork made of swamp ash faces the atrium just as a bouncing ball between the ceiling and floor, leaving the curving path freely.

A tier of light and bright serigraph glass boards has covered the surface. Some wide and narrow stripe patterns are printed tightly and orderly. As the location changes, the function of the glass boards will change accordingly. When the window is covered, it is like a tier transparent board which is for preventing sunlight. On sunny days, all of the boards will turn down to the horizon level and then people will be able to enjoy the beautiful scenery outside.

The last architectural element to be introduced is the "box", which is inserted by boards and comprises 3 small guest rooms. It is located between the glass quartz spheroid and the square base, nearby is the great gate. Since this "box" extends for about 8m from the building, it seems to be suspending above the ground.

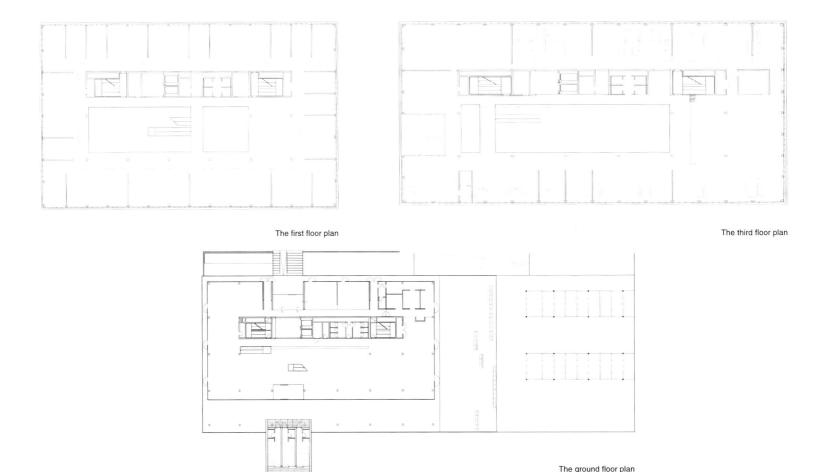

The first floor plan

The third floor plan

The ground floor plan

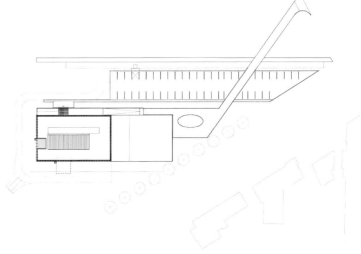

The orientation plan

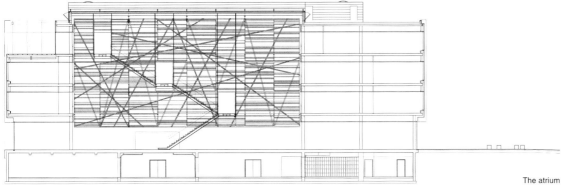

The atrium

Location Ettlingen, Germany
Architects Behnisch, Behnisch & Partner
Photos Christian Kandzia

New Administration Building of Entory AG

The New Administration Building of Entory AG is located at the north of Ettlingen in Germany. It covers 15 000 sqm and was used as a part of Rhineland Barracks. In the north, there is a big orchard which connects with the eastern Black forest mild terrace. It becomes the door of Ettlingen Town because of the special geographical location. It is also connected to the neighbor speedway. All of these are the main characteristics of the place.

The clients need a multi-functional construction, in which offices can be built for individual, associations, open-plan office. Then, the staff would be able to choose most suitable woking ways according to their own requirments. The construction also needs a central space for meeting and it will help the staff to integrate into society.

This place is a transition belt from populous cities to villages. In order to avoid a kind of huge and self-enclosed style, the architects have chosen an open and independent style that grows from the constrcution center and integrates into the nearby landscape.

Architects made use of a gentle staircase to raise up the entrance. It leads to the multi-level, resplendent and magnificent entrance. In the other side of this project, the

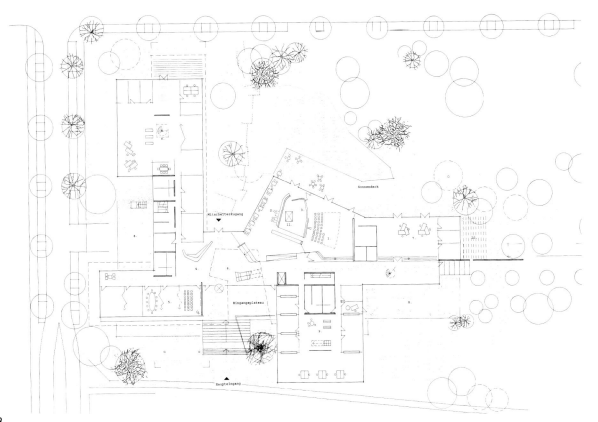

1 boardroom
2 dining–room
3 pantry
4 gateway
5 information room
6 passage to exhibition
7 leisure area
8 flat roof
9 working area
10 corridor
11 cenacle staircase

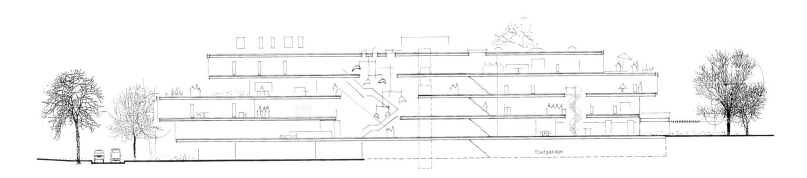

Tiefgarage

garden will be viewable. The dining room and the meeting room face the garden. Some removable walls separate these areas with the lobby, which is convenient for holding large scale activities.

The independent buliding wing of the colligate building is connected with the lobby. And in the lobby, the meeting room, offices, lounges and the other spaces are distrib-uted on different floors. It also includes a communication zone, the exhibition hall and the footbridge. Moreover, the nearby open staircase connects different floors to form the functional and spatial connection.

The elevation that faces the Karlsruher street has simple structure and is quite traditional. However, another elevation that faces the black forest is open and the style integrates with the natural environment—the colors of the fences complement the nearby lawn and trees. The screen wall, which is made of transparent organic materials, makes the color effect more vagarious under the shiny light, and change infinitely.

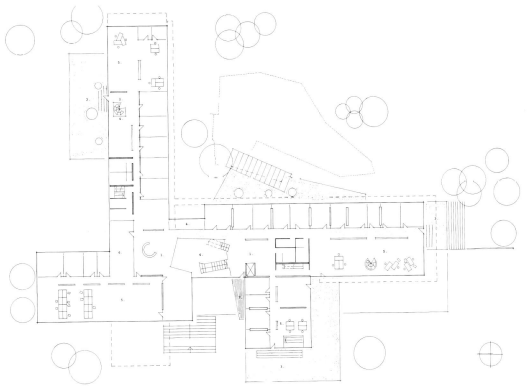

1 exhibition/reception/central office
2 pantry/tearoom
3 flat roof
4 outdoor space
5 office
6 muniment room
7 balcony

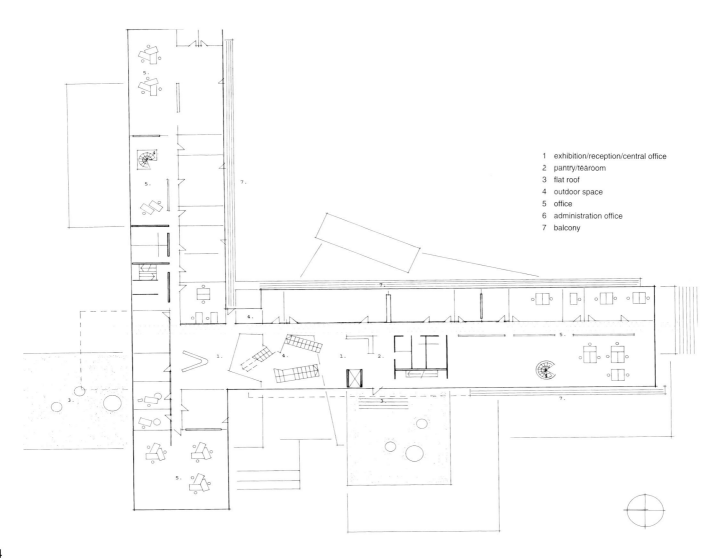

1 exhibition/reception/central office
2 pantry/tearoom
3 flat roof
4 outdoor space
5 office
6 administration office
7 balcony

Architects   Rafael Vinoly Architects PC

Photos   Brad Feinknopf

Plan and chart   Courtesy Rafael Vinoly Architects PC

The New Graduate School
of Business of University, Chicago

The setting of the Chicago University is composed of a series of squares, which creates a remarkable characteristic in this college and shows a unified feeling. The aim of the architects is to design the new Business Graduate Teaching Building to be a public space, and to encompass all functions of the university in it The whole square yard is surrounded by a "greenhouse" which can be used all year, and can serve as a passage in the main hall. The way how the buildings assembled is determined by the functional standard as well as its relationship with the peripheral environment.

In the plan, the new building goes parallel with the Ida Noyse Hall and forms a little shade trail which not only connects both sides of the square yard but also hides the garage ramp. The main entrance matches well with the Ida Noyse Hall and also strikes a balance with the Rockefeller Chapel's Mini–corridor. Each floor has been constructed backwards to match with the scale of the nearby construction and reduce the stronge feeling when people look down to the streets. To reduce the vertical moving of students and visitors when they enter the main entrance, horizontal design is used in the design plan. All facilities of the students' centre are arranged on the first floor. A multi–receipt is directly open to the Winter Garden central functional zone, so that the goal of unifying all functions is achieved.

The teaching facilities are concentrated underground which is close to the entrance base. The natural sunlight from the Winter Garden and reaches the square yard centre through a 3–storied circular space. The reading room, which surrounds the circular space,

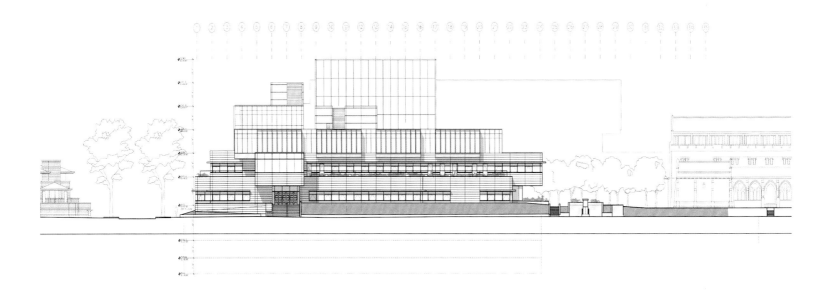

making use of the natural light. A computer laboratory is located at the center of the plan. The distance between the computer laboratory and classroom, the distance between the computer laboratory and other teaching facilities are the same. The administration and student admissions centre is on the second floor, which is used as a functional layer and a gap between the students and teachers' space. Students' activities have to take place on the third, fourth and fifth floors. The purpose of such settings is to increase the girth and avoid the office settings being too undiversified. The surrounding scenery and service area are viewable from all offices, while the Winter Garden can be seen from the central office. An independent office is built around the service area and fixed in a series of suites. The setting of the suites makes the whole design more private and intimate.

The construction connects the open staircase vertically. These 3 major floors include the student center, and the teaching facilities underneath, and the administration and students admissions centre on the upper floor. All of these surround the Winter Garden and connect all the floors of students, teachers and staff, as well as the public areas.

The Winter Garden acts as the communication center, and is the light source of the entire internal part of construction. It is also a place where different kinds of ceremonies of the university are held. The architects referred to the style of Rockefeller Church tine arched window when they design this building, and it creates a feeling of pointing to the sky directly. The neighbor construction's elevations are divided into two layers. The darker part is wrapped into a horizontal

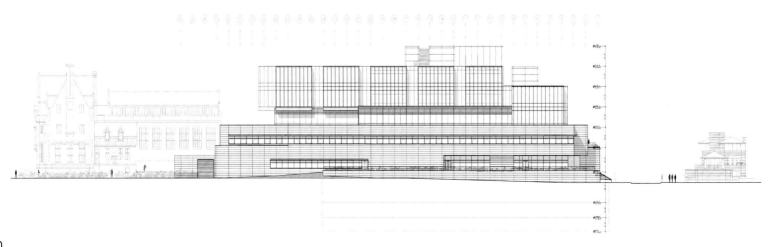

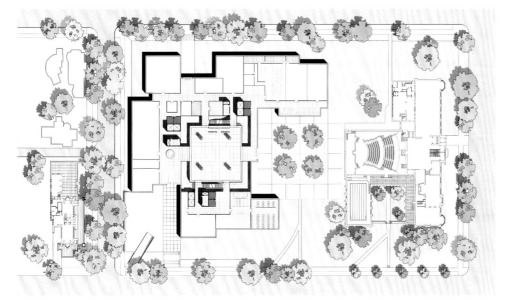

limestone board and forms the scale of the building, echoing with the horizontal plan of Robie House. The upper and backward-facing part of the office is light in color, which faces the glass screen wall. Hence, people could enjoy the beautiful scenery on campus through the screen and could use a more lager roof terrace.

The design proposal follows a clear structure and an energy-saving principle, and the style is never repeated. The roof is designed according to the impregnable gothic style logic, by using transfer of strength of tiny structures. It is composed of 4 tube-steel components. The tiniest vault rib frame is connected with some thin horizontal structures. An arc surface can be found in the structure. A thin carved frame is connected to the arc surface which could block sunlight. The elegant column creates an imagination of the branches in the garden. The filler shape of the vault appearance makes the rain fall into the four column's center and then into a reservoir. When it snows, the pressure created will not be exerted on the vault but on the columniation. The concave surface of the ceiling accelerates the speed of hot air transfer and leads the air into the roof directly. Hence it makes the indoor ventilation can be maintained all year.

The building method is to strengthen the dialogue between the two big subjects of this project—the heavy characteristics of the construction of the edge as well as the bright color tracery of the central building. All buildings in the university have a consistent style. The quality public spaces show the reverence and prudence towards studies of the university.

Clients Commissioner City of Rotterdam, Dienst Stadstoezicht (STZ) Commissioner City of Rotterdam, Ontwikkelbedri jf Rotterdam (OBR) Commission Via European selection

Location Veranda strip, Feyenoord, Rotterdam

Architect Architectenbureau Paul de Ruiter b.v.

Construction consulter ABT adviseurs in bouwtechniek b.v., Velp, the Netherlands

Underground park area 350 m²

The ground park area 300 m²

The first floor stores area 500 m²

The first floor bar and restaurant area 500 m²

Completed and using time 2005.9

Photos Rien Van Rijthoven

Veranda Parking Garage

The parking Garage makes people feel free. In the past, the design of car park usually does not consider the design of the entire building. Passengers and visitors' safety is not taken into consideration either. So, if there is a good arrangement for car park, the habitability and safety of a city can be shown. Car parks like the Veranda have become a business card for the environment. On the roof, drivers enjoy such beautiful scenery which an automobile cinema cannot possess.

The area next to the Rotterdam's Feyenoord Stadion has a lot of apartments, stores, bars and large cinemas. It provides 630 parking spaces for neighboring inhabitants and visitors, and providesthem high efficiency. The ground floor is actually located at the middle of the building, and is designed as bars and restaurants. According to the limitation of the building as well as its goal of creating 630 parking spaces, the design has to begin from the underground. The most important beginning is that it creates a humanistic parking garage which provides a bright, joyful and unique environment and evokes the kind—heartedness of people. The parking garage has 9 floors, 4 of which are underground. With the aid of translucent external elevation, structure plan and construction method, the dispersed sunlight passes through the voids in the middle of this 9—floor building, arriving at the originally dark basement, filling the car park with open characteristics. The abundant sunlight makes the car park become a clear and ventilative place.

The concept of the car park is floating activity. The floors upon the ground are connected with each other and inclined upwards. In the gyrating road, you can reach the

ground straight from the roof. In order to connect the under-ground floors, a declining road is constructed in the building. The climbing lines on the outside elevation make the movements seeable from the elevations. And at the some time, in order to strengthen the concept of shape, the upper structure is designed as an upward twisting curve surface which plays a major role in the expressiveness of the construction; yet it also complicates the entire structure.

The complexity of the construction also exists in this area. This area used to be a wharf and is polluted, so the groundsill can not be dug too deeply. A project team composed of architects, the construction company, geological technicians and installation consultants have worked out an integrated designing plan, which carries out the latest technology to perfect the functions. For instance, it mocks a fire condition by using computers and installs a 35m high screen wall on the floor by renovation skills. They have also made use of a method that enables the walls to be set in their own positions on the underground floors.

The elevation of the building is made of special metal plates. These metal plates provide the parking garage with natural ventilation and thus people can enjoy the distant scenery outside. In order to realize the special folding and opening of the thin steel, the experts had invented a new product which is still strong even it is holed. The building looks as if it is made up of thin steel boards. During nighttime, the light which goes through these holes makes the building surface particularly attractive. People from the outside are able to see the people and cars inside, which are moving up and down. The design, shape and materials used in the building can attract people's attention no matter at day or night.

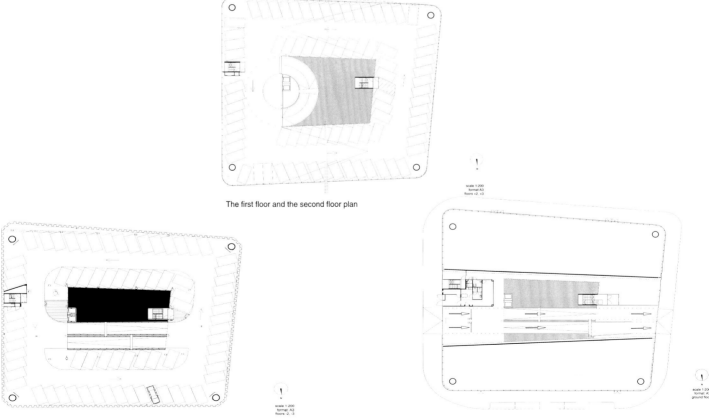

The first floor and the second floor plan

The underground second floor and underground third floor plan

The ground floor plan

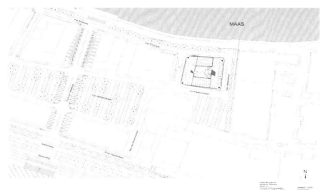

The orientation plan

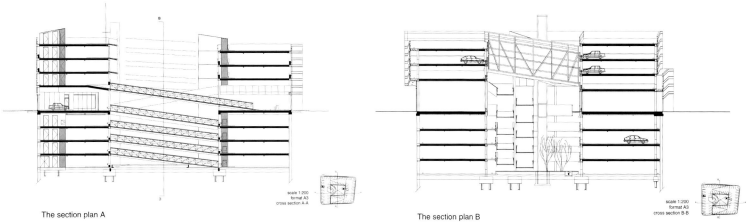

The section plan A

scale 1:200
format A3
cross section A-A

The section plan B

scale 1:200
format A3
cross section B-B

Clients	Denver International Airport
Architects	Leo A. Daly, Los Angeles
Project designer	Alex Ward
Project manager	William R. Hebinck
Project architect	Ric Ramos
Structure engineer	Art Hansmire
Consultant	K.T. Architecture P.C.
Civicism structure	S. A. Miro, Inc.
Engine & electric	BCER Engineering
Electric	Roos Szynskie
Surroundings	Rowan Williams Davies & Irwin, Inc.
Photos	Courtesy Leo A. Daly, Los Angeles

New Terminal Canopy for Denver International Airport

The unique design of the new Terminal Canopy of waiting building in Denver International Airport takes into account innovative designs and safety of the passengers. The pair of canopies has a length of 244m, and is designed according to the theory of aerodynamics. It has been awarded the excellence grant by Industrial Fabrics Association International. The innovative superexcellent steel structure also obtained an outstanding award by the American Institute of Steel Construction.

The terminal canopy is designed by Los Angels Leo A. Daly Architecture. Leo A. Daly comprises the best airports designers from all over the country. This project involves the design of a pair of transparent canopies, with a length of 244m. The designing concept conveys a feeling of fluttering and highlights the complete design of the airport. At the same time, the canopies serve as a shelter for passengers who are waiting for bus or taxi on the ground floor in the rain. An extended traffic lane on the 6th floor provides a designated taxi stop for passengers and ensures the safety of the passengers.

The new architectural element perfects the canopy structure of the 9 years old airport

building, and it also becomes a symbolical architecture in that City. "The design of canopy matches with the roof of the waiting building, which is covered with an elongated strong cloth, and creates a bright and pleasant sensation." Just as the designing general inspector, Mr.Alexander M. Ward said, "the passengers can easily notice the Mt. Rocky framed by the man-made canopy once they step out of the building." The canopy, located at both sides of the 5th floor of the central building, is supported by a tube structure which is tied by external steels. The outer surface is covered by a transparent fabric. The canopy is approximately 12 375sqm. Mr.Ward also drew our attention to the facade of the design, "the white fabric extends up to the sky and it looks like a pair of wings, creating an image of a flying bird. It also makes people think of a model plane made in early times." The sustainability of the environment is also a major concern in this design. The transparent cover allows abundant sunshine and fresh air in daytime; and during nighttime, its illumination facility brightens the entire canopy from the lower floor to the entire waiting building.

"The project was restricted by a number of factors during the designing process," said the design manager of Denver International Airport, Mr. Reginald Norman, "We must highlight the uniqueness of design of the 5th floor canopy, and at the same time, it must match well with the roof of the waiting building. We also have to avoid blocking the view from the pavement of the 6th floor." Finally, Leo A. Daly managed to complete the project design and construction within a limited budget.

Hotel Haeckenhaus

Haeckenhaus Hotel is an extended building on the original foundation of the Forelle Hotel. It was built next to a small artificial lake in Easugefarze. The hotel is located on the dam and integrates with water. In the hydraulic engineering permission's scope, the south–ern part is connected closely with the lake. The design of this project is to highlight the direct relation between the first floor and the lake. The path linked to the lake was built of a series of kinds of materials, such as wooden boards, graveled path and wooden fence which make up the ending part of the pathway.

The main construction is located at the west of the dam. It advances towards the dam and ends on the second floor, such that a small path leading to the swimming pool on the lake can be built. A lot of plants on the tower's roof connect the building with the beautiful scenery. The sunbath room is clear and simple. There are no three–dimensional models, and the windows are installed on the outer surface of the existing construction. The design, which is mainly based on the existing architecture, manifests naturally the differences

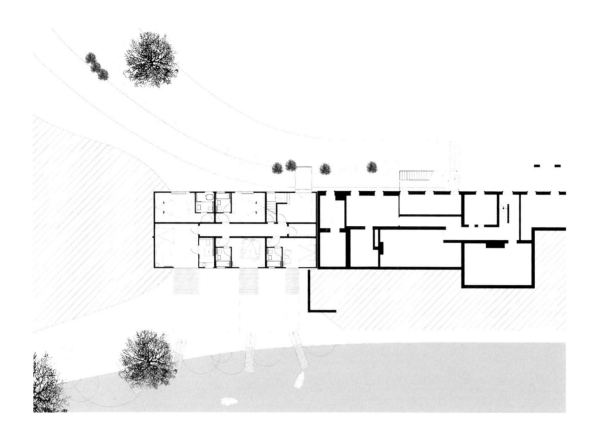

Wasserstand= OK Schwelle

Ansicht von Süden (Eiswoog)

Neubau Hotel ◄ ► Bestand Landgasthof

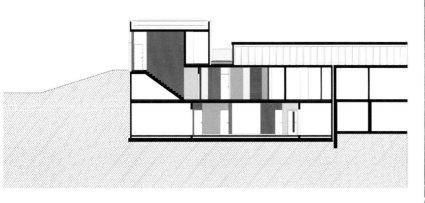

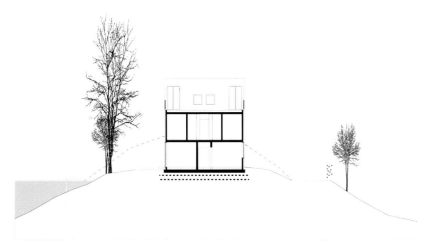

between the new and the old. The existing roof extends to the new building and ends at the tower.

In front of the Forelle Hotel, the board fences are raised up on the gravel foundation and extend to the entrance of the hotel; it forms a natural connection between the old front desk and the entrance of the new hotel. Guests enter from the special–designed entrance. The walls were de-signed with a series of colorful plans, and colors were cho-sen based on the design of the corridor, doors, switches, fire–alarm, fire extinguishers and some decorated symbols. The color of each independent room also follows the color designing. Moreover, the designer pays attention to bathroom's integration with natural landscape such that the one who is bathing is able to enjoy the lake scenery. Windows are not of the same size. Hence, beautiful land-scape elements such as the horizon, rivulets, railway bridges and forests could be immerged into the space. The design of guest rooms is simple and clear, and a black adsorption gum Arabic floor and bright Birkenholz furni-ture have been arranged therein.

Location Mexico City
Designer India Mahdavi
Photos Lisa Kerry

Hotel Condesa, df

The hotel of Condesa df, located at the center of the entire Condesa df area, is also at the center of Mexico City. It is a place which people are bound to visit when they come to the city. The purpose of this project is to build up the brand image, so the designer started off with naming the project. Hotel Condesa df, which is named after a local place, expresses the concept and implication of the "headquarters" of the region appropriately. The Condesa df area is a place in the Mexico city where pop art is most active. The extraordinary architectural facade of the Art Nouveau, the streets filled with comfort and green spaces make people feel free and joyful. In the past ten years, a lots of bars, galleries and restaurants have been built there.

There are 40 guest rooms in the hotel. Since 1928, the Paris style construction has stood at the entrance of the branchy street. It faces the beautiful Espana park and the design of hotel portrays a non-ordinary style of freedom and relaxation. The classical furniture designed by India Mahdavi establishes the main tone of the entire hotel—simple, charming, filled with fashionable and popular elements.

From bars to the reception room, from restaurant to the ballroom, and from court-yard to the terrace, a brand new concept of "lift is art" appears everywhere in the hotel.

Passing the central lobby, all activities are displayed surrounding a shaded courtyard with flourishing plants and the courtyard is designed with reference to the Mexico Manorial style. Each floor of the hotel has installed walked-terrace, so people can overview the internal courtyard. The Persian blinds installed along the terrace floor filter light and integrate the light and shadow organically, producing a contrast of light and shade which makes people feel pleasant.

The guest rooms satisfy the visitors' sensual satisfaction and provide a resting and relaxing place within the fast-pace life in Mexico City. The high roof in the room, the walnut wooden bed head boards facing the window, the blooming Jacaranda mimosifolia under the window and the handwork carpet from Oaxaca all add rich local characteristics to the room. All of the products and materials are 100% natural.

If visitors want to relax themselves after a long and tiring day, they could go to the gymnasium near to the hotel which contains perfect fitness facilities. At the same time, a boxing class, Turkish sauna bath and an outdoor hot spring are arranged in the activity room of the hotel.

Location   Toronto, Ontario, Canada
The designing team   Siamak Hariri (Partner in Charge) Jaegap Chung (Project
                        Manager), Francis Lapointe, Steven
Structure engineer   Bauer, John Cook, Liming Rao, Dennis Giobbe
Engine engineer   Blackwell Engineering
Electric engineer   Toews Engineering
Soft landscape   Dynamic Designs Engineering Inc.
Hard landscape   Janet Rosenberg+Associates
Water construction   Hariri Pontarini Architects
The main contractor   Dan Euser
Photos   Richard Wilson Management
The area   Steven Evans, Hariri Pontarini Architects
Completed   1 180 m²
                        2005 spring

Art Collectors' Residence, Toronto

This house is located at the suburb of Toronto. The design exhibits the expression of modernism as well as the sensitive reaction it has towards the nearby landscape, making it an extraordinary building. This 8 000sqm built-up area, which is surrounded by tall pines, forms a natural enclosure. This double-floored house is located at the central of the land. It is leaning towards the front, as if it is floating between landscapes. Its "L" shape divides the broad land into three parts, while remaining the connection between two parts unobstructed.

The architect's inspiration of design comes from the master's collections of artworks. The house is not just for daily accommodation, but also for spa and gallery show, hence it is full of shinny & transparent sensations, just as the feeling that water and sunshine give. The interior design has satisfied the master's enthusiastic pursuit of art: it not only has the house acted as a place in which he keeps his collections of vivid artworks and furniture, but it has also reflected his healthy lifestyle. For the external design, the architect made good use of the materials in designing, so as to match the design with natural landscape, and to blur the boundaries between external and internal, simplicity and complexity, tradition and innovation.

The living room is located at the centre of the house, which could solve the problem of the contradicting natures between the master's bedroom and other public areas like the art gallery and spa. The lower floor of this house is almost transparent, so it does not contain any private rooms. However, since the upper floor of the house is not transparent, private spaces be arranged everywhere. The internal designing is full of surprises: there is a rather broad and round room in which the door can hardly be seen, so that people could look through the whole room from one side to another, and from the inside to the outside.

The gallery covers the low and the upper two floors. Its ventilation windows and roof windows are allowing lights in to protect and lighten the collections. What is most eye-catching is the round-shaped staircase, which is like a sculpture extending straight up the roof. The spa area includes a gymnasium, a sauna room, a swimming pool and a massage pool. The area surrounding the massage pool is decorated with limestone boards, which form a bridge connecting the pools from its inside to its outside.

The water in the outside pool falls from the interlayer to the lower part of the pool, and continues flowing from the fountain of the mini-waterfall to another side, bringing a sense of silence to the entire

house. The circulation of water is also applied to the ceiling designs of the gallery and swimming pool – the wave–liked ceiling resembles falling water droplets, forming sharp, wavy lights, floating on top of your head.

The sunshine permeates through the ventilation windows, skylights as well as the French windows and falls on to the solid white walls and French limestone and walnut wooden floor. The lights brighten the house, creating a cheerful and lively feeling, as if one is floating in the sky freely.

For the external design of the house, architects have paid extra efforts to create a "architectural language"–to match the construction with natural materials, such as A'er Gang limestone, details made of bronze, penthouse, oak or teak window, and the little anteverted waterfall fountain. The plants in the waterfall fountain give people a sense of perpetuation, naturalism and permanence.

30 NOVELTY ARCHITECTURE

Copyright © 2008 Liaoning Science and Technology Publishing House

Asian edition published in 2008 by Page One Publishing Pte Ltd
20 Kaki Bukit View, Kaki Bukit Techpark II, Singapore 415956
Tel: [65] 6742-2088, Fax: [65] 6744-2088
enquiries@pageonegroup.com, www.pageonegroup.com

First published in 2008 by Liaoning Science and Technology Publishing House

Editors: Qiaoxin Ye, Yuyan Zhang
Translator: Yuan Duan
Layout & design: Fangfei Zhou
Cover design: Dexian Feng

ISBN 978-981-245-763-9

Printed and bound in China